The Divine Commitment

Partnering with God
to Change Your Life

Mark Furlong

⊕ Strategic Book Publishing
New York, New York

Copyright © 2009 Mark Furlong. All rights reserved.
No part of this book may be reproduced or transmitted in any form or by any means, graphic, electronic, or mechanical, including photocopying, recording, taping, or by any information storage retrieval system, without the written permission of the publisher.

Strategic Book Publishing
An imprint of AEG Publishing Group
845 Third Avenue, 6th Floor—6016
New York, NY 10022
http://www.strategicbookpublishing.com

ISBN: 978-1-60860-017-5, 1-60860-017-3

Book Design: Bruce Salender

Printed in the United States of America

Dedicated to Janet;
you are the love of my life,
second only to Jesus.
Thanks for loving me on my transformation journey.

Introduction

Even though a God-connected life is potentially the greatest life possible, far too many are not enjoying it because they are stuck and not making real progress. Despite experiencing the life changing power of Christ in real and wonderful ways, barren spots or deep ruts of the soul can be stubbornly difficult to overcome. It can be confusing even knowing which approach to take. Do we "let go and let God" or do we "fight the good fight and take hold of eternal life"? If, despite real and sincere efforts, no progress is made, apathy, discouragement, and hopelessness can drain the life right out of God's people.

What if, instead of focusing on our limitations and our failures, we focused on the power and faithfulness of our Creator? What if we came to realize that the one who has the power to envision, create, sustain, and guide a universe in the fulfillment of his eternal purposes has made an awesome, divine commitment to us? God has made a commitment to finish what He started in us, a commitment to fulfill His purposes in our lives, a commitment to shape us into the image of His son, Jesus. When that becomes our focus and we learn to draw on the resources He provides, new levels of transformation can be reached.

The Divine Commitment comes out of the author's thirty years of working through this issue of change and transformation in his own life, as well as with others, both in the U.S. and overseas. God is always at work in us, doing far more than we are ever aware. He changes us in some areas with no or little effort on our part. Yet, there are regular times when He wants us to specifically partner with Him to see transformation occur. Focusing on God's willingness and ability to finish what He started in us, He intends these to be hope-filled, faith-building, limit-busting processes that will help us be and do all that He has intended. To that end, He has provided some wonderful insights and resources to help us make genuine progress.

No book can cover everything on a subject, especially one this vast. This book does not address major psychological or developmental issues (at least not directly). It also does not address those amazing, spectacular, revival type transformations that really do happen in history and in our own personal lives from time to time. It does not endeavor to reach people who have no desire to change. The focus of this book is for people who sincerely want to grow and change, but they are having trouble doing it. God has made available to every one of us the resources and processes for life transformation. We just need to learn what they are and how to follow God on the journey.

The Divine Commitment is divided into four main sections: Platform, Power, Process, and Practices. The chapters are intentionally short so they can be read for just a few minutes or for longer periods if so desired.

Introduction

The Platform section focuses specifically on God's ability, commitment, and desire to help us change, even when we have failed. It also shows how God's truth is foundational for lasting change. As a matter of fact, without God's truth, lasting change cannot happen. Truths for transformation that can be remembered and built upon are included here.

The Power section tells us more about the Jesus who came to change the world. He absolutely loves helping people break out of old patterns and into His new ways. He is actively working in each person's life to do far more than they ever could on their own. He knows the time, the events, and the experiences each person needs to go forward. He gives us the Holy Spirit, who has the power to break us out of ruts and lead us effectively, according to God's plan. His Word gives us guidelines for recognizing the Holy Spirit's leading, so we can focus on His plan at His time.

The Process section teaches how God works to bring positive change. To cooperate with Him, we need to understand the key points of how He does it so we can work with Him rather than against Him. Faith is a key ingredient in growth, but it is not meant to be a heavy, "have to do absolutely everything just right" burden. Rather, Biblical faith is a life-giving virtue that enables a person to stick with it for the long haul and to resist the enemy's attempts to bring them down.

The Practices section gets very practical, describing how to use certain types of prayer for life transformation. God's presence is the most important element in anything positive happening in life, and prayer is the main way to live in His presence. All types of prayer are helpful in shaping us into the image of Jesus, but certain types of prayer have proven especially beneficial in the process. Those are covered here.

Basing one's life on God's faithfulness, love, and power always produces positive change. *The Divine Commitment* will encourage, enlighten, inspire, and challenge readers to get in the river of God's purposes and fulfill all God has planned for their life.

Contents

Section I—The Platform 11
   Chapter 1 Life Change Is Possible 13
   Chapter 2 You Can Learn the Walk 21
   Chapter 3 Realization Leads to Liberation 30
   Chapter 4 Foundational Realizations 40
   Chapter 5 Changing Your Theme Song 50

Section II—The Power 61
   Chapter 1 Jesus the Life Changer 63
   Chapter 2 Rut-Busting Holy Spirit Power 74
   Chapter 3 The Mind and the Holy Spirit 84
   Chapter 4 Following God's Lead 95

Section III—The Process 107
   Chapter 1 How God Works 109
   Chapter 2 Receiving from God 117
   Chapter 3 Dealing with Delays 130
   Chapter 4 Dealing with Our Enemy's Schemes 140

Section IV—The Practices 153
   Chapter 1 Changing through Prayer 155
   Chapter 2 Prayer Planning 168
   Chapter 3 Prayer Pictures 179
   Chapter 4 Prayer Proclamations 188
   Chapter 5 Prayer People 200

References 213

Section I—The Platform

Chapter 1
Life Change Is Possible

The God of the Bible is a hope-giving, life-changing God. His Book is filled with genuine accounts of people who positively changed. The stories of the patriarchs in Genesis tell us of Abraham being transformed from a man who gives in to fear and cowardice, betraying his wife on two major occasions, to a man who becomes the "Father of Faith." Isaac, Abraham's son, gave in to the very same temptation as his father. Still, he became such a man of influence (even though he was a stranger in a foreign land) that the leaders of that area wanted to make a treaty with him because they saw that God was with him in whatever he did. Isaac's son, Jacob, turned from being a lying cheat into the man after whom God's people would be named. All of this was just in one family tree. Page after page of the Old Testament tells us stories of people who changed in wonderful ways.

Section I—The Platform

Once we get to the New Testament and Jesus comes on the scene, the pace quickens considerably. Wherever Jesus went, things changed. He would go into a town and incurably sick people were made well. People with heavy spiritual, social, and psychological needs were liberated. The rejected, the poor, the "down and outers" as well as the "up and outers," and the sinners were all powerfully, authentically, positively changed through encounters with Jesus Christ.

The first words Jesus taught carried the hope that real change was possible. After Jesus finished His preparation and testing time and began to publicly bring God's message to people, Matthew 4:17 (New American Standard Bible) tells us, "From that time Jesus began to preach and say, 'Repent, for the kingdom of heaven is at hand.'" The Greek word, "repent," translated here means to turn around or change your mind; to go in a different direction. It has a radical edge to it, meaning a huge change is necessary and possible. Some have made it out to be a negative, oppressive word (mainly by the tone of voice they use or speaking with a condemning attitude), but it is actually a great, hope-filled word. At the core of Jesus' message, He is telling us we can really change, we can repent and experience a whole new way of life with God as our leader and provider. Jesus knew and taught that people needed to change and could change.

Since the time Jesus lived in Israel, the pace has not slowed down one bit. If you have already received Jesus Christ as your leader and sin-forgiver, no doubt you have a story, probably many stories, of how God has already worked wonderfully in your life. One of the joys of serving as a pastor is to see those changes and to hear those stories on a regular basis. In my thirty years of following Christ, I

Chapter I • Life Change Is Possible

have never once met someone who has truly received Jesus who cannot tell me stories of how their life has positively changed.

Because every follower of Christ has experienced God's life changing power to some degree, we know, at least in theory, that continued transformation is possible. We know God is alive and well and His power has not faded one bit over time, so we should be able to continue on our journey of transformation decade after decade. We realize if God could change us as much as He already has, then more change is certainly possible. Yet, far too many eventually reach a point where they consciously or unconsciously begin to think they really cannot change past a certain point. Spiritual growth seems to stagnate. God may seem far away. The same old mistakes and sins are repeated over and over again. Despite confessing, praying, pleading, or making sincere and solemn promises, an invisible wall has been hit and it is not moving. When a person keeps ramming into an immoveable wall, it is easy for passivity or hopelessness to set in. It hurts to hit a brick wall with all your strength. If a person has no other tools to use, then a common response is to begin to say, "I am just going to have to accept this. This wall is too high for me to climb, too thick for me to break through, and too long for me to walk around. I am going to have to live with this sin or spiritual deficit." Instead of experiencing a vibrant, enthusiastic, hope-filled life, wonderful people, people that God loves, get weary and doubtful, becoming survivalists rather than victors.

There are obviously some things about us that will never change in this lifetime. We will never grow past a certain height. Our basic personality and gifts will not change and neither will our past. Whether good, bad, or

Section I—The Platform

neutral, there is nothing we can do about those things; we do have to accept them. However, there are also some positives that will never change, which we can use to break through those seemingly immovable walls.

God's love for us never changes. He loves us as much today as He did when He took our sin on the cross. Paul wrote in Romans 8 that there is nothing that can separate us from the love of God. God's basic will for us never changes either. The Bible says He thought about us and laid out a plan for our lives before we were ever born (Psalm 139, Ephesians 1:4, New International Version). He formed us according to His sovereign will, giving us the right gifts, abilities, personality, birthplace, country, and even the right time in history, to fulfill His purposes. He surely does not scrap those carefully designed plans because of some obstacles, problems, or even failures on our part. For God, nothing is too hard.

Let's focus for a moment on the phrase: "God's basic will for us does not change." It does not matter how long you have been stuck behind that wall, how long you have battled that problem, or how long you have been spinning your tires; God's will for you has not changed. Revelation 22:1-2 (NIV) gives us a brief but impressive picture of one aspect of the spiritual world: "Then he showed me a river of the water of life, clear as crystal, coming from the throne of God and of the Lamb, in the middle of its street. On either side of the river was the tree of life, bearing twelve kinds of fruit, yielding its fruit every month; and the leaves of the tree were for the healing of nations." You might need to read that passage a couple of times to get the picture clearly in your mind. This passage talks about the tree of life bearing constant fruit and bringing healing.

Chapter I • Life Change Is Possible

If you remember the story of Adam and Eve, the tree of life was present even back in the Garden of Eden. When Adam and Eve chose to eat of the wrong tree, the tree of the knowledge, of good and evil, instead of the tree of life, all of creation changed. Adam and Eve's nature changed, the force of sin and death entered our world, and the devil was given authority to cause great damage. Yet, the last book of the Bible describes this tree as still being present in God's plans. This tree is not just present; it is also available despite Adam's sin and ours. God's will for mankind has never changed. Life, fruitfulness, and healing are still His will for us and always will be.

There is also a river in this passage. A river is constantly flowing with water; otherwise, it is no longer a river, but rather a pond or a lake. It has to have sufficient size and power; otherwise it is called a creek. I am so glad God said there is a river flowing from His throne, not just a little creek. A river does not stop; it keeps flowing with incredible power and influence. The same is true of this spiritual river. It flows from God Himself, carrying His life, power, wisdom, and purposes, and it never stops or dries up. God's river is constantly coursing from His throne to bring life and to accomplish His will wherever it goes.

Here is the great news for us, even if we have hit a dry spot where we are not experiencing abundant life right now, or we have messed up and gotten out of the river for a while and we are sitting on the banks, there is still hope. Maybe we have been hurt, disappointed, or rejected and have stepped out of God's flow. The river is still flowing. It does not stop. It never changes. Certainly, there is a cost to living out of God's river. We do miss out on that part of the journey, or we live that part of our lives in dryness rather than in the blessings God wants to give. But if we turn back

Section I—The Platform

to Him, or get back in the river, or adjust our course so we are not fighting the current of His will and start to go with the river's flow, we are immediately back in God's will for our lives. I have seen this so many times over the years. For whatever reason, people have never gotten fully into the river, or they have decided to sit on the bank for a while. They are missing out on what God is doing or wants to do in their lives. But as soon as they get back in the river, God's unchanging grace and power are there to carry them on their journey.

Our heavenly Father has committed Himself to us and He will not stop working in our lives. He will not quit. That is why Paul could write, "For I am confident of this very thing, that He who began a good work in you will perfect it until the day of Christ Jesus" (Philippians 1:6 NASB). Paul saw the perfecting and the transformation of our lives, as a work of God. A work God has committed Himself to completing. Ephesians 2:10 tells us we are God's workmanship, His masterpiece, and He is carefully, patiently, beautifully doing His work in us.

If the God who knows all things and has the power to create a universe has committed Himself to working in us and perfecting us, what should that do for our level of hope? If we realize He will not quit, and we believe He will finish what He started, the needle on our hope gauge will rise dramatically. We will begin to shake off the weights of apathy and discouragement that try to hold us down, and we can press through the lies that try to keep us out of the river. We will hear our heavenly Father call to us with these words, "Come on in, the water is great! Let's go on this journey together. It is time to jump into the river of life and let your soul be refreshed. You do not have to be afraid and sit on the banks or stay in shallow water. I will be with you

Chapter I • Life Change Is Possible

every second. Let My power carry you as you learn to swim and navigate in the river of God." It does not matter how dry or weary you have been, or how long you have been sitting on the riverbank, the river is still flowing for you.

When I was serving as a missionary/pastor in Munich, Germany in the '80s, a man named Tom started attending our church services. He made an appointment to come and talk with me, and as we sat in my office he began telling me his story. During the 80s, there was a hit show on prime time television called *Dallas*. For those too young to remember or who never watched the program, it was an evening soap opera. The most famous character was a ruthless, snake of a man called J.R. Ewing. J.R. was a merciless, deceiving, greedy, cruel character who used and abused people for his own personal gain. Nothing was too low for him. So, it was quite a surprise when Tom started our conversation with these words, "I have been in the business world for many years and I have done the worst things imaginable. You know the show *Dallas*? I make J.R. look like an innocent little kid." He paused quietly for a moment then continued, "Would Jesus really take someone like me?" I told him, "No way, you're too rotten!" I'm just kidding. I told him about the cross and how Jesus absolutely loves to save sinners like him and me. A short time later, he made the decision to receive Jesus and I watched as this man began to change. He started reading the Bible, coming to church regularly, and looking for ways to get involved. It was such a joy to watch his entire countenance change, going from hardness to love, heaviness to joy. And he became such a servant.

When the Iron Curtain of communism fell in the late 80s, along with the joy of newfound freedom, there were

Section I—The Platform

also many needs in those eastern European countries. The communist governments were not good, but they provided at least some basic services and stability. With those governments suddenly gone, there was a huge hole in meeting the basic needs of the people. Our church, along with many others, looked for ways to help. Tom was our champion in this cause. He organized the gathering of food, clothes, and medicine. He put teams together that loaded the goods onto trucks and took these important items to Romania. He led several expeditions in the heart of winter, often going to the smaller towns where few others were helping. He and the team came back telling us how little, desperate, barefoot children came out to the trucks in the snow. They told of the looks of joy and gratitude on the faces of the people as they received life-sustaining goods. A few years later, Tom met a woman in the church who had also experienced God's grace. They married and are living positive, loving, contributing lives. Despite living for decades as a hard, merciless man, Tom changed dramatically. He stepped into the river of life and God's power and grace were available to carry him on the path God had ordained for him. A man, who once used his management and leadership skills for selfish gain, had become a force for good in the world. If you know the God of the Bible, you know He loves doing things like that in and for people.

The same God who has already done some great things in your life has committed Himself to completing it. He wants you to be fruitful, to experience and demonstrate Christ-like character, and to do meaningful works that help change the world. His river is still flowing. The tree of life is still available. Life change is possible!

Chapter 2
You Can Learn the Walk

I had hit another one of those walls in my spiritual journey. I wanted to change, I really did, but I kept making the same old mistakes over and over again. Don't get me wrong, God had changed me significantly in many areas of my life. Looking back, I, my wife and kids, and those around me could be truly grateful for the changes that had taken place, and continue to take place, in me. A natural skeptic and one who could easily see the glass half empty rather than half full, I had become much more positive, hopeful, and faith focused. I had become more loving and joyful than I had been earlier in my spiritual journey. I was making a difference in the world through my ministry. Yet, there continued to be certain areas of my life that just didn't seem to respond like they should.

I am no great gardener, and don't really care to be. Having a perfect lawn is not one of my main priorities in

Section I—The Platform

life, but I do try to keep it looking decent to be a steward of what God has given me and to be a witness to my neighbors. However, there is this spot in my lawn that is barren. Even though I have fertilized, watered, planted seed year after year, and a couple of times I've even aerated it, this one spot continues to remain barren. Surrounded by lush grass, in a safe and loving environment, it still refuses to grow. There were areas in my life that were that way also. I have a wonderful wife and two sons I am proud of and really enjoy. I am consistent in my devotional times, and always have been; I particularly love Scripture and worship. Sometimes I would fast (probably not as much as I should, but I do it in streaks) and I was trying to live an obedient, godly life. Yet, when I looked on the lawn of my soul there were these obvious bare spots and it was really frustrating.

Scripture encourages us to "add to our faith" goodness, knowledge, self-control, perseverance, godliness, brotherly kindness and love (2 Peter 1:5–7). Peter continues God's instruction, in verses 8 through 10 (NASB), "For if you possess these qualities in increasing measure, they will keep you from being ineffective and unproductive in your knowledge of our Lord Jesus Christ. But if anyone does not have them, he is nearsighted and blind, and has forgotten that he has been cleansed from his past sins." I wanted to be one of those who had these qualities in increasing measure. I wanted to be effective and productive and I sure didn't want to be nearsighted, blind, and forgetting that I've been cleansed from sin. Yet, in some important areas I wasn't "adding to" and my spiritual lawn had this enduring, noticeable bare spot.

I have been in pastoral ministry long enough to realize that I am not the only one. Most people I know really do

Chapter 2 • You Can Learn the Walk

want to change and grow. Studies tell us most of us are very aware of areas of bareness, areas that need to change but do not. In his book *Primal Leadership* (2002, 95), Daniel Goleman reports that even many top executives, people who were high-achievers, known for great confidence and performance, did not believe they could really change in certain areas of their lives. If these people, who have changed entire organizations, sometimes entire markets, felt incapable of changing, this view has got to be prevalent with a majority of us. Yet, one of the great encouragements of Scripture is that we *can* change.

I had experienced *some* real and positive growth, and continued to experience it, but …those lousy bare spots. What could I do to get fruitful? Over the years I tried a couple of main approaches. With some modifications from time to time, the first could be called the "abide" or "rest in God" emphasis. Jesus said He was the vine and we are the branches, apart from Him we could do absolutely nothing of true value, but staying connected with Him or "abiding in Him," we would bear much fruit (John 15:5). Jesus made it perfectly clear that the only way to really grow and change is by the life and power that flow from Him. Colossians 1:27 tells us that "Christ in us is the hope of glory." Galatians 2:20 says, we've been crucified with Christ, and now Christ lives in us. This is the New Testament focus, dependence on Christ in us, around us, and with us to live fruitful lives.

I heard people rightfully teach, "You cannot do it on your own. Quit trying and start trusting. Jesus' yolk is light and His burden is easy. Rest in the Lord, be still and know He is God." That is absolutely correct. We cannot save ourselves, we need a Savior, and His name is Jesus. We do not want to fall into the trap Paul strongly warned the Galatian

Section I—The Platform

Christians about and try to finish in our own strength what God started in the Spirit, by His grace and power (Galatians 3:1–5). So I was giving it my best to "abide" and "rest" in God's finished work. I would consciously pray and remind myself that God is the One doing the work. I would fellowship with Jesus by reading and meditating on His words, worshiping, praying, and then basically trusting Him to do it. Like a drink of cool water on a hot day, it was very refreshing and very encouraging because the pressure was off. My thinking was, this was God's work and He will complete it if I just give it time. So I gave it time, actually a lot of time over the years, but even with some good results, there were still noticeable barren spots in my soul.

Once again, let me clarify. I'm not talking about a little character development that will eventually happen, but if and when it happened would not affect other people very much. I'm not talking about being perfect either. I'm talking about barren areas that are important, areas that impact the lives of people around me. As a husband, I was not being loving or affectionate enough to make the most wonderful person in the world feel loved and appreciated by me. I wanted to be more proactive and encouraging in raising my sons. I wanted to manage my moods well enough that I would not bring a cloud of heaviness home with me after a tough day. I wanted to get motivated enough and actively and regularly share the good news of Jesus with people around me. Those are the types of things I am talking about; important areas of life that were not just impacting me negatively, but also the people around me. Those were parts of life I knew I should be addressing, and theologically, biblically had the power to do, but just saw little, if any, improvement.

Chapter 2 • You Can Learn the Walk

So at different times, I tried the second major approach. The other side of the coin, we can call the "pressing on" emphasis. As inspirational speakers have said, "If it's going to be, it's up to me!" Paul did write to "forget the past and press on to the high calling of God in Christ Jesus" (Philippians 3:12–14). He said to train like an athlete so we could compete in such a way that we win the race (1 Corinthians 9:23). God told Joshua to rise up and go take the land. Jesus told us to "Go into the whole world" and preach the gospel and disciple the nations. These and many other Scriptures are action-oriented, personal responsibility-focused truths. I realized there was an action component and God was not going to do it all for me. He expected me to be actively involved in the process.

With this in mind, I made my vision statements, wrote down my goals, got some accountability partners, revved up my internal engine, and said, "I'm going to take the land. I am going to change!" And it was great! My wife, Janet, commented on how much more loving and positive I was. I was sharing my faith with more people and some were coming to Christ! I was more upbeat, faith-filled, joyful, and really enjoying the progress. It was good, exiting stuff …for a while. After a few months, however, I found I wasn't able to keep it going and I noticed myself sliding back into the old "barren spot" way of living again.

No doubt about it, change is not always easy. On top of dealing with the guilt of not growing like we desire, we also have to deal with confusion about the right approach and battle hopelessness when we do not make progress. Do we "rest and abide" or do we "fight and resist"? We've had good experiences in abiding, but not enough results fast enough. I know, some of you are thinking, Mark, your problem is not abiding *enough.* Give it time and it will

Section I—The Platform

work. I think you're right, if we understand abiding in the right way, which I will talk more about later. We've also had good experiences in exercising a "rising up, pressing on, the violent take it by force" attitude. Those of you who are action-oriented may be saying, "Quit being such a wimp. It's your job to keep yourself in the faith and to govern your own soul." You are right, too. I should shoulder some of the responsibility here, yet I, and many others, just have not been able to keep it going at a high enough level. So what's the answer? I think it is a wonderful blending we can call partnering with God.

Ephesians 6:10 (NASB) describes it well, "Finally, be strong in the Lord and in the strength of His might." Paul talks about it again in Colossians 1:28–29 (NASB) when he says, "We proclaim Him, admonishing every man and teaching every man with all wisdom, so that we may present every man complete in Christ. For this purpose also I labor, striving according to His power, which mightily works within me." Here is this beautiful blending that God wants to take place. This is how He designed us to operate. It is not one or the other; it is both "abiding" and "pressing on." We are strong, but not in our own strength, rather we draw on God's strength. We "labor" or "strive," according to God's power which works powerfully in us. We take action while depending on God's grace, realizing we can do nothing of real benefit without Him. We also give Him our best effort, trusting Him to empower us and help us do what we cannot.

Let me give a few illustrations on how this works. In 1831, a brilliant scientist, who was also a devout Christian, named Michael Faraday made a world-changing discovery. Through his experiments he realized that "whenever a magnetic force increases or decreases, it produces electric-

Chapter 2 • You Can Learn the Walk

ity; the faster it increases or decreases, the more electricity it produces" (Guillen 1995). This realization changed the world because it made the development of dynamos possible. Dynamos, in turn, made never before seen amounts of electricity available, and made it available to the masses. We entered into the age of electricity. A completely new dimension of advancement and improved living was made possible because of the power made available to us. The source of this power was the increase and decrease of magnetic force.

What does that have to do with partnering with God? I think there are great similarities (not perfect correlations). One force would be "abiding," the other would be "pressing on." If you have ever been to a power plant, even though there is noise it is more like a hum, not a clacking, grinding, "something is falling apart" noise. When the generator is running as it should, it is smooth and fairly quiet. It is running at a high speed, increasing and decreasing with such ease, that it just sounds like a hum even though tremendous power is being produced and released. But the first dynamos did not work nearly that well or produce near that amount of power. As with all inventions, many mistakes were made in the experimentation and developmental phases. There were times when awful grinding sounds came out of the machine, where it did break down, and where very little power was being produced. It took a lot of time and experimentation, or practice, to get it right. Partnering with God is also a learning process. At first, we do one or the other, we "rest" or "fight," and it can be awkward and confusing. There are short-term successes followed by breakdowns, lousy results, and repeated failures. However, the longer we walk with God, these two "forces" start working together in a smoother and more rapid fash-

Section I—The Platform

ion, until, after a while, it is hard to distinguish them. A beautiful hum begins to be heard and great power and results occur with relative ease. When there is a stressful time, a time when more power is needed, more can be drawn. When less power is required, the demand can be decreased, but there is this constant blend that produces much more power than one or the other by itself.

Let me give another simple example. Walking involves two legs. When we first start walking, it is a real struggle. I've never heard of a child who just stood up and began running with perfect form and ease. Small children wobble, they fall over, and they strain to maintain balance. Even when they master standing up, they still walk funny. Like mini Frankensteins, they move with stiff legs, teetering back and forth, usually good for a few laughs. With time, everyone who has healthy legs, hips, etc., begins walking naturally and fairly effortlessly. Most of us do not stop and think, "Now, left leg you go …right leg, wait a moment. Okay, now right leg, you go." It really does become natural and relatively easy. Do we still have to be aware of what we're doing? Yes. Do we still have to draw strength and energy from outside sources such as food, water, and air? Of course we do. Yet, walking becomes a normal, natural, easy way of life and it takes us places far beyond where just hopping on one leg could ever do. It is the same in making real progress. Several times the Bible uses the phrase, "walk with God" or "walk in the Spirit" as a description of how God designed us to live. He has given us the ability to both "abide" and "press on" by understanding and practicing both concepts.

These two forces, abiding and pressing on, help us to "be strong in the Lord and in the strength of His might." (Ephesians 6:10) As we realize God created us to live this

Chapter 2 • You Can Learn the Walk

way and then begin to practice both approaches, great power and grace are made available to help us change and grow into the people we want to be. We can see once barren spots become full and lush. We learn the walk that enables change to occur.

Chapter 3
Realization Leads to Liberation

My father-in-law grew up in a small town in northern Alabama. One day, when he was five or six years old, he went with his father to the local drug store, where his father made a purchase. At the counter, the owner asked how he wanted to pay and his dad said, "Put it on my tab." The store owner said, "Good enough," and they walked out the door with the purchased item. When my father-in-law saw that transaction, a light went on. A short time later, he went back to the drug store and ordered a milk shake at the ice cream counter. When it came time to pay, you guessed it, he said, "Put it on my dad's tab." The store owner knew them both well and thought it was funny, so he did it. Well, you can imagine what happened next. My future father-in-law began inviting all his buddies to go get free ice cream and milk shakes. Groups of little boys joined him on a regular basis to enjoy free ice cream. When his dad got the

Chapter 3 • Realization Leads to Liberation

bill at the end of the month, they had a man-to-man discussion and the "put it on my tab days" were put to an end. Nevertheless, for a period of time, realization had led to liberation.

Some of the most quoted words of Jesus are, "you will know the truth and the truth will set you free" (John 8:31 NASB). God's truth liberates us, sets us free, and changes us in remarkable ways. That is why Scriptural teaching, preaching, reading, and learning have always been, and always will be, important for life transformation. There is no way around it. If we really do want to change, knowing God's truth is irreplaceable.

When I was a young Christian, I would read the gospels and wonder why Jesus spent so much time teaching. With all those needs around Him and power flowing through Him to heal, set free, and meet needs through His touch and words of command, why did He take all that time to teach? In some of the meetings I attended where the leaders were going to pray for people, I would ask myself the same question, "Why are you taking so long to teach what the Bible says? Just do it already." I wanted the action, not the words. I wanted to see some lives changed right now, without all the Scriptures and comments. The longer I am a Christian though, the more I see that God's words, His truths, are among the main instruments He uses to change us. Without realization of truth, lasting change is not possible. God's words are the substance He used to create the universe and it is the substance He uses to change us.

When reading the Old Testament, I was puzzled at how the children of Israel could see with their own eyes some of the greatest miracles in the history of the world and still not "get it." They not only saw the miracles, they had the personal experience of walking through the parted Red Sea,

Section I—The Platform

eating manna from heaven, and seeing a cloud of protection by day and a pillar of fire at night. Still, they slipped back into the old way of living over and over again. One of the main reasons they kept falling was they did not receive God's truth into their souls; they did not allow it to sink in. They heard it, but did not receive it. Even the greatest experience, without a base of truth, will not last. Jesus said it is like building a house on sand, it will not hold up under the pressures of life. But if we realize and receive God's words, we build God's substance into our souls and we can survive, grow, and excel even when the storms of life hit.

That is why Paul would take so much time to teach, preach, and write. When God's truth is realized, change and liberation happen. Truth carries amazing power, but it only produces results in our lives if it is known. My father-in-law had ice cream and milk shakes available to him all his life, but he never experienced them in abundance until he saw the truth about how things work. It is the same with us. In His love and wisdom, God has already provided "everything that pertains to life and godliness" (2 Peter 1:3) for us. It is already in our spiritual account in Christ and will be released to us as we progress on our journey of discovering and doing His will if we can see it.

Genesis tells us the stories of the patriarchs Abraham, Isaac, and Jacob. When Jacob was born, the second of twins, he was grabbing on to his brother's heel. In those days, people were named according to how they were seen, whether positive or negative. Since he was born holding on to his brother's foot, he was named Jacob. Jacob sounds like a fine name and we hear it often, but it means "deceiver, cheater, or one who supplants." How would you like it if every day, every time someone called your name, it was in such a negative light? "Hey Mrs. Rebecca, can De-

Chapter 3 • Realization Leads to Liberation

ceiver come out and play? Deceiver, come and help me clear the dishes. Cheater, let's go to work."

Not surprisingly, Jacob lived up to his name. He tricked his brother out of his birthright as the first-born son, a big deal in those days. He then tricked his father into giving him his brother's blessing, an even bigger deal. Jacob stooped so low that he tricked his own father into giving him something holy, something that belonged to his brother. That would be like breaking in and stealing from a church to get God to bless you. Crazy. When Esau, Jacob's brother, heard about this, he threatened to kill Jacob once their father, Isaac, had died. He meant it and he was definitely the type guy who could do it. So, under his mother's guidance, Jacob headed out on a long journey, alone, to spend some time with her relatives until Esau cooled off.

On this journey, Genesis 28:11 (NASB), describes the beginning of Jacob's turn around, saying, "He came to a certain place and spent the night there, because the sun had set; and he took one of the stones of the place and put it under his head, and lay down in that place." Talk about being in a hard place; he is sleeping with a rock for a pillow. Jacob is alone, he has been caught in his trickery, and the consequences of it are catching up with him. If he has any conscience at all, it is really bothering him right about now as he is forced to look back at his life thus far and where it has brought him.

But in this dark, hard, and lonely place, God gives Jacob a dream. He sees heavenly activity, with angels ascending and descending on a ladder from heaven to earth and back again. God speaks to him and tells him that He is the same God who interacted with his grandfather and father, giving them great promises for the future. He reaffirms those promises to Jacob and promises to be with him.

Section I—The Platform

Jacob awakens from the dream and says, "Surely the Lord was in this place, and I did not know it." He was afraid, and said, "How awesome is this place! This is none other than the house of God, and this is the gate of heaven" (Genesis 28:16–17, NASB). Jacob then turns this place of hardship into a place of worship, which is a great response.

When you read the rest of his story, you see that Jacob still had a lot of change ahead of him, but this was the turning point. From this time forward, he was on a different path. God already had a plan for Jacob. Even before he was born, God told Rebekah (his mother) that both he and Esau would become nations and that Jacob would end up stronger than Esau. God was already watching Jacob and had great plans in store for him. However, Jacob was still living according to his fallen nature, trying to manipulate things to his advantage, rather than seeking and trusting God. When God gave him a dream, when God showed him his truth, when Jacob *realized* God was with him, the liberation process began. Jacob's response was, "God is here, in this place, He is involved in my life, even in the lowest and hardest of times; and I was not even aware of it." Realization leads to liberation and transformation.

This is how it works in our lives as well. Because of the pride we all deal with, it often takes shake-up times before we face our "Jacob" nature. When we see the awfulness of our sin, it is easy to feel like a total loser; alone in our dark, hard place. But when God's truth comes, when we realize more of what He is like and the plans He has for us, those old chains begin to loosen and fall off. Sometimes it is a huge, dramatic event; most of the time, it's a little at a time. Nevertheless, the realization of God's truth leads to liberation in our lives.

Chapter 3 • Realization Leads to Liberation

The biblical word for realization is *revelation* and that is what Paul taught us to pray for on a regular basis for ourselves and for others. In his letter to the church in Ephesus, Paul included a powerful prayer that he prayed for them on a regular basis. He prayed that God would give them a "spirit of wisdom and revelation in the knowledge of Him, …that the eyes of your heart may be enlightened, so that you will know what is the hope of His calling, what are the riches of the glory of His inheritance in the saints, and what is the surpassing greatness of His power toward us who believe" (Ephesians 1:19–23, NASB). Of all the things Paul could have included in his letters, have you ever wondered why he included the prayers he prayed? There are a couple of good reasons:

1. By including these types of prayers, Paul was teaching Christians how to pray; something every disciple, starting with the twelve, wanted to learn how to do.
2. Paul used the written prayers as teaching tools to help us see what God's will for us is. By seeing what, and how, Paul was praying, we all see to a greater degree what God has made available to us through Jesus.

Through Jesus, God has opened up a completely new realm of life. In Jesus, we have already been blessed with every spiritual blessing in the heavenly dimension (Eph. 1:3 NASB), but it does us little or no good until we realize it. Our computers have the capacity to do amazing things, but we can never take advantage of what the designer put into them until we know what is possible and know how to access it. It is the same with spiritual riches. That is why

Section I—The Platform

Paul prayed repeatedly for a "spirit of wisdom and revelation." He prayed that the spiritual lights would go on and that we would *know* the wonder of God and all He has provided for us. When the lights go on, the experience will eventually follow.

When we truly realize what Paul is praying, we are liberated from empty, confused living because we know God's purpose and calling for us. We are liberated from the fear of not having enough because we know God has provided a rich inheritance for us that touches every area of life. We don't shrink back from life's challenges, because we know God's great power is aimed towards us for good. When we realize God's truth, we can't help but experience liberation and positive change!

When I was in Germany, I read a brief newspaper article regarding a woman in Hamburg. In Germany, like some cities in the U.S., there are open markets everywhere. One day the owner of a fruit stand had had enough for the day, so he put out a sign on the front of his stand that read, "Free Fruit. Help yourself," and he left. At first no one took any fruit, they thought they might be stealing or they were wondering what the catch was because, after all, nothing in life is free. Eventually an elderly woman cautiously went up to the fruit stand and took one piece of fruit. She looked around to see if anything would happen to her. When nothing did, she began taking more, still looking to see if she was going to get in trouble. When nothing happened, she then began loading up all her shopping bags. Others saw this, and in just a few minutes the fruit was gone. Once the crowd realized the truth, "the fruit is free," their lives changed and improved a little bit more as quality food was provided for them.

Chapter 3 • Realization Leads to Liberation

Not everyone sees God's truth, however. Many people walk right past the fruit stand and live spiritually hungry lives because there are a couple of essential conditions for spiritual enlightenment to occur:

1. Humility. In Matthew 11, Jesus had just rebuked some of the cities where He had done most of His miracles, yet they did not respond. Verses 25 and 26 (NASB) continue by saying, "At that time Jesus said, 'I praise You, Father, Lord of heaven and earth, that You have hidden these things from the wise and intelligent and have revealed them to infants. Yes, Father, for this way was well-pleasing in Your sight.'" God is actually pleased to hide His truth and riches from people who think they are smarter and more intelligent than Him. The Bible is clear—God resists pride because it is a root of so much sin and because of the evil it produces. Pride actually blinds us to God's truth.

    God loves humility, though. Jesus said the Kingdom is made available to the "poor in spirit" or the humble. His love and power flowed freely to those who realized they needed God, but not to those who thought they were in such great shape that they needed no Savior. He gives grace and revelation to the humble.

    What does it mean to be humble? It does not mean hating yourself or letting other people step all over you. It does not mean thinking less *of* yourself; instead, it means thinking less *about* yourself. It means, in your heart and mind, you bow down to God and say, "You are God and I am not. I yield to You, realizing Your wisdom, knowledge, and

power far exceed mine. The smartest thing I can do is to believe You and follow Your instructions." This attitude allows God to teach us and show us His incredible riches.
2. Hunger for God and Truth. Jesus said, "If you continue in My word, then you are truly disciples of Mine; and you will know the truth and the truth will make you free" (John 8:31–32 NASB). The word "continue" indicates an ongoing pursuit, not a casual, hit and miss, once a week at church approach. Proverbs 2:5b tells us that a person who searches for wisdom and truth like treasure will "discover the knowledge of God." God has wisdom, insights, and knowledge stored up, waiting to be accessed, released to the person who continuously seeks to know Him and His ways. 1 Corinthians 2:9 tells us that God has things prepared for us that are beyond what our minds can conceive and they are prepared for "those who love Him."

    It makes sense, doesn't it? God wants to reveal His heart, His nature, and His riches to people that truly value Him. His guarantee is that, if we seek, we will find. God will reveal His truth to us and that truth will set us free. That is what so many others and I are experiencing. Looking back over my walk with God, seeing God's truth and receiving it into my soul have been the greatest forces for change of anything I've experienced. Every now and then God performs a dramatic, instantaneous work of grace in my life, but by far the greatest percentage of positive change that has happened in me has come through revelation of His words. Realization will

Chapter 3 • Realization Leads to Liberation

lead to liberation and positive change in all of us; knowing the truth really does set us free.

Chapter 4
Foundational Realizations

Every now and then, I go to a professional football game. Last fall, my son and I were privileged to actually go down on the field before the game started and see the players warm up first hand. A couple of things stood out to me as we watched them get ready. First, these men are extremely big, strong, and fast. You know they are, but when you see them up close and personal, you get a new "revelation" of it. Second, I noticed that even though they are playing the game at a much higher level than a normal human being ever could, the pregame drills they were doing were basically the same as I had done in Little League, high school, and college. These exceptional athletes, using much more complicated schemes, plays, and coverages than a high school team, still did the same basic drills to get ready to play. What is true of professional football players is true of us as well. No matter how good we get, we can never get

Chapter 4 • Foundational Realizations

away from the basics; fundamentals are important. In education there are core concepts and classes we must grasp and pass to master more complicated or advanced subject matter. In football, a player never gets away from the basics of blocking and tackling. In spiritual growth it is the basics of the spiritual disciplines: Bible reading, meditation, study, prayer, worship, fellowship, service, and evangelism. These are key areas we will always need to practice in order to progress.

There are also some essential realizations that I think are critical to partnering with God in life change. We need to get these firmly planted in our souls and then come back to them from time to time so that we can stay on track. Hebrews 2:1b (NASB) tells us "we must pay much closer attention to what we have heard, so that we do not drift away from it." If you have ever goofed around on a raft or a boat, you know they can easily drift. My wife, Janet, tells the story of falling asleep on an inflatable raft in the water at a Florida beach. When she woke up she was a long way from shore. When she fell asleep she was close to the beach, but when she woke up it was shocking how far she had drifted. It did not take any effort at all; the raft was just carried by the current. In case you had not noticed, there is a spiritual current we all deal with in this world, which can easily carry us away from God and His truths if we do not pay attention. Far too many people wake up one day and discover they are in deep water, far away from where they want to be, and they cannot figure out how they got there. They just went with the flow of the world and drifted. However, drifting away from God will not help us change the way we want to. When we just drift with the spiritual currents of our world, they eventually bring us to dangerous waters. To make sure we stay on course, we need to make

Section I—The Platform

sure that we pay attention to some solid, fundamental truths for transformation.

The first truth has to do with God's nature. God is so big, so deep, so wide, and so high that it is not only difficult to describe him fully, even with the richest of vocabularies, it is impossible. Someone brilliant and powerful enough to design, create, and run a universe from the smallest molecule to the largest sun, who has always existed and always will, who knows every hair on the head of every person who ever lived, is beyond our mental capacity to fully comprehend. That said, for the purpose of life change, there is a one-sentence description of the nature of God, which Jesus gave his disciples, that is the best summary statement I know. Jesus' closest friend and follower, John, wrote, "This is the message we have heard from him and declare to you: God is light; in him there is no darkness at all" (1 John 1:5 NIV). I love meditating on that verse because, with just a few simple words, we get a picture of God that is accurate, deep, and impacting. Jesus said this is the message His followers need to proclaim, "God is light; in him there is no darkness at all." That means God is good to the core. There is not the slightest trace of evil in Him. There is no jealousy, no bitterness, no lust for power or fame, or anything else for that matter. He is never tempted to do something unjust or unrighteous. He never lies and His desires for us are always motivated by love. As the great worship song goes, "God is good all the time, all the time God is good." He is absolutely perfect in every way. He is holy, joyful, peaceful, courageous, gentle, and strong, with no flaws whatsoever. On and on it goes, "God is light; in him there is no darkness at all."

Why is this so important for life change? Romans 2:4 tells us it is the kindness and goodness of God that leads us

Chapter 4 • Foundational Realizations

to repentance (or change). Ephesians 3:19–20 (New Living Translation) says, "May you experience the love of Christ, though it is so great you will never fully understand it. Then you will be filled with the fullness of life and power that comes from God." Seeing God as good, seeing His kindness and receiving increasing amounts of His multi-faceted, multi-dimensional love is what helps us change into the kind of people He created us to be. It actually causes us to be filled with "the fullness of life and power that comes from God" Himself. As Blaise Pascal rightly said, "We all have a God-shaped vacuum" that only God can fill. God made us to fill us, and He wants to fill us with Himself, especially with His love, which is beyond our comprehension.

I do know people who have come to Christ as a result of a real revelation of hell and judgment. They saw the rightful end result of their lives if they did not turn to God and, thankfully, they did. They came to Jesus and were relieved of that terrible and real fear of spending eternity apart from God in a place of torment. Even in cases like these I still do not know of anyone who keeps growing into a God-loving, people-loving, Christ-like person, who does not focus often on God's love and goodness. Love is the greatest force in the human soul, not fear. Fear can drive people to action, but it will only go so far. 1 Corinthians 13 tells us that love will never fail, it will never quit, it keeps on going. God is love, and whatever comes from God overcomes the world.

Everyone grows and blossoms best in an atmosphere of love, acceptance, and encouragement, not accusation and blame. A critical, judging environment actually shuts us down, causing us to close up and put up protective walls. We move into "turtle mode," hiding in our shells. But as

Section I—The Platform

the saying goes, "A turtle only gets ahead by sticking out its neck." We only grow when we open up, and we only really open up in a loving, safe environment. That is the environment of God, the one He has made possible through Jesus. He is light. He is good. He shows love and acceptance far greater than any human being can. He wants us to come with open hearts and minds to a secure place, where we can let Him love us and work in us and with us.

Because of our sinfulness, we do need tough love and discipline from time to time, but love is still the key word. My wife and I practiced loving discipline with our kids, including controlled, brief spankings. When our oldest was born, we read an article that bank robbers are often very intelligent and determined. We are convinced, because of his incredible determination to do what he wanted to do, his high energy, and keen mind, that our oldest would have been out robbing banks by now if we had not diligently and lovingly warmed up his backside from time to time. Because we loved him and really did want the best for him, we disciplined him. We did not run a boot camp or a home filled with lots of rules and punishments. Loving, encouraging, and accepting each other was the main focus. As a result, we have wonderful sons who have turned into great young men. The oldest is not robbing banks; he just finished college and is excelling in life as he follows Jesus. The youngest is also a godly young man, who finished high school this year and wants to make his mark through vocational ministry and possible missions work. It did not happen because Janet and I were, or are, perfect, but because we focused first on God's love and goodness.

It is the same with you. You will not feel free to be honest about your struggles, to come and confess your sins, to come to God for His help, if you believe He is going to

Chapter 4 • Foundational Realizations

hammer you every time you do. But if your soul is being filled with the love He has for you, there will be a desire to change and live a life that is pleasing to Him and good for the world. Oh, I pray that each of us would be able to see God smile at us and hear him tell us how much He likes us and is for us. That realization and experience is a must for God-empowered transformation.

That leads us to the second essential growth truth—the truth of grace. The rest of this book is going to examine the principles, truths, concepts, and practices that will help us break through barrenness into fruitfulness. However, it only works the way God intended when our focus is on God Himself and we look to Him for His grace to do what we could never do on our own. Grace is defined as "unmerited favor," something freely given as a gift. It is not something we work for or something we earn. Scripture tells us we are saved and made right with God by grace. The abilities God gave us are a result of his grace, as are the manifestations of the Holy Spirit. Paul said God's grace gave him the ability to work harder than others. The book of Acts further tells us that great grace was on the church and, as a result, there was great change and impact.

In our pursuit of change, it is important to lean heavily on God's grace. It is foundational to realize even if we never did change, because of His grace given through Jesus, God still accepts and welcomes us. I once heard a man say, "God loves you just the way you are. He also loves you too much to leave you that way." Some people, because change can be slow and difficult, think God must be sick of them already. When they believe that, they end up turning away from God and His love. That response is pretty common for those not yet anchored in grace because it is so often how our world works. If we perform well, we

Section I—The Platform

are accepted; however, if we fail or do not perform up to people's expectations, we are rejected. Rejection is incredibly painful and to feel rejected by God is the worst rejection of all. So, it is critical to remember that none of us were ever good enough to earn God's love or forgiveness. Perfection is God's standard. He cannot let even one sin into heaven, because if He does it will not be heaven anymore. It is only by trusting in Jesus Christ, and what He did for us on the cross, that any of us is made right in God's sight. It is by grace that we are saved, and it is by grace that we continue to come to God and receive His soul-filling love. It is in an atmosphere of grace that we continue to grow and change.

<u>Grace lifts the pressure of perfection off of us.</u> From time to time I have had to change a flat tire. Even though I work out on a regular basis and have fairly good physical strength, if I had to lift my car and hold it while someone else changed the tire, I would end up in the hospital with hernias and a messed up back. But if I use a jack, it takes on the weight of the car so I can easily change the tire. I still have to loosen the bolts, take off one tire, and put on the other, but it is so much easier because of the jack. Grace lifts the weight off of us so that we can do our part without the crushing weight of having to be perfect. Please make that truth an anchor in your heart. We are people of God's grace because of Jesus.

The third change producing truth we need to realize is this—when we receive Jesus as our Lord and Savior, our spirits are made brand new by God's Spirit. 2 Corinthians 5:17 (NIV) says, "Therefore, if anyone is in Christ, he is a new creation: the old has gone, the new has come!" Every time a person comes to Christ, God does a miracle in his core and in his spirit. God replaces that dead, stony heart

Chapter 4 • Foundational Realizations

and replaces it with one that is alive and receptive to Him. That is a reality and it happens every single time a person is converted. Yet, we still do not live perfectly because we have to learn to live with a new spirit and that takes some time and practice. Our souls (mind, will, and emotions) are not made new at conversion, only our spirit is made completely new. Our souls have to be renewed, released, and restored. That is why we all still have areas of our lives that are not the way we want them to be. Ephesians 4:24 (NASB) says, "...and put on the new self, which in the likeness of God has been created in righteousness and holiness of the truth." Our new self (in our spirit) has already been recreated by God and, in the very likeness of God, is righteous and holy right now. This is absolutely true. However, Paul wrote that we still need to "put on the new self" in our thinking, decisions, and emotions.

I have a neighbor who restores cars. Every time I walk by his house, he is working on some type of automobile. It would be silly for him to do all the body work and make the outside of the car beautiful if he never replaced the engine. The engine is what gives the car its power to actually go someplace. When we receive Christ, God puts a new engine inside us; the old one was dead. Then He starts working on the rest of the car, restoring it and making it into something beautiful. The car can already go forward. It can take us places even if the upholstery and radio and paint job are not finished. It is a work in progress, but the car restorer will not be satisfied until it is all done. God has given us a new inside, but the outside is still being restored. If you understand this, it will help you when you read all those powerful, past tense and present tense statements about who we are in Christ throughout the New Testament. In our spirit, at our core, we are right now who those words

Section I—The Platform

say we are, but in our souls, much repair, renovation, and renewal must still take place.

The fourth truth I think is foundational for partnering with God is this—focus on progress, not perfection, in this life. If you know the Bible, you could say to me, "Doesn't Jesus tell us to be perfect, just as our Heavenly Father is perfect? Aren't there other Scriptures that tell us to be perfect?" Yes and yes, but there are also other Scriptures like 2 Corinthians 4:16, which tells us that our inner man is being renewed day by day, and 2 Corinthians 3:18, which tells us that we are being transformed from glory to glory, and 1 John 1:9, which tells us that if we sin all we have to do is confess it to God and He will cleanse us from all sin and unrighteousness. God is going to make us perfect and free from all sin, but that will not fully happen until we get glorified bodies at the resurrection. Until then, we can keep making progress for as long as we live. As long as we are living in God's love, grace, and truth, we can keep improving. That is so encouraging to me because I love progress and I know, physically, a person can only develop so far. You do not see eighty-year-old men setting world records in speed or power events, but spiritually we can keep growing and progressing as long as we live. Some areas of our lives will be more developed and stronger than other areas, but Jesus said that we could expect, at the very least, a thirty-fold increase in every important area of our lives. As we grow in grace, there exists the very real possibility of much more (Mark 4:20). That is a great deal!

Sometimes it can get discouraging if you look at how far you still have to go to become like Jesus, but it is very encouraging if you look at how far you have already come. A great thing to do from time to time is to stop for a moment and reflect on what your life used to be like compared

Chapter 4 • Foundational Realizations

to now. People are generally amazed at the improvements that have taken place. As we've already talked about, the God who has already done some impressive things in your life up to this point is going to continue that process. He will never give up on you because He loves you enough to die for you. In His love He has laid out plans for you much greater than you would ever come up with on your own. They are not necessarily greater as our world defines "greatness," but in terms of how God defines it, HIS plans are much greater. You just need to make sure you do not give up on Him, or on Him working in and through you.

No book can cover everything on a subject, especially one with as many variables as life change. Though the foundational realizations we have just covered in this chapter are referred to, and implied, in the following pages, I felt it would be good to take a few moments to spell them out clearly, though briefly, before going on. I will not always specifically mention them in the following pages, but know they are foundational for the help God gives in helping us grow and change. Pay attention to these four anchor truths and you will not drift; you will have a solid base from which to build. Let us look at one more before we move on to the Power to change in Section II.

Chapter 5
Changing Your Theme Song

There is something almost magical about a song. It touches our emotions like few other things can and it helps us to remember words, events, and experiences to a far greater degree than we would without it. Even though I am not a musician and have no musical expertise, I can sometimes identify a song I listened to years ago just by hearing the first few notes. An upbeat song can give me a lift, a contemplative song can help calm me down, and worship song can help me encounter God. There is great power in a song.

Let's try a fun little test. I'll give you the name of a television show and you try to hear its theme song in your mind. You can even sing it or hum it if you like. *Gunsmoke ...Bonanza ...Hawaii Five-O ...All in the Family ...Cheers ...Seinfeld ...Friends ...24 ...CSI* (whichever one you want). Your age and the amount of television you have

Chapter 5 • Changing Your Theme Song

watched may well determine how many you know. But, if you are living anywhere within the borders of the United States, over 99 percent of you will know at least some of them. Each show has a theme song that tries to communicate to us the main emphasis, idea, or feel of the show. It works, too. When most of us hear one of those theme songs, our minds readily shift to some aspect of that show: the name, a scene, a character, for example. Just as each of these shows has a theme song, so does the kingdom of darkness and the kingdom of God. Whichever theme song we learn and live will determine the content of our lives. If we want to partner with God for life change, we need to learn heaven's song so it can become our theme song. What is the song of God's kingdom? Let us read Revelation 5:9–10 and 12–13 (NIV) and then I'll explain:

"And they sang a new song: 'You are worthy to take the scroll and to open its seals, because you were slain and with your blood you purchased men for God from every tribe and language and people and nation. You have made them to be a kingdom and priests to serve our God, and they will reign on the earth …Worthy is the Lamb, who was slain to receive power and wealth and wisdom and strength and honor and glory and praise.' Then I heard every creature in heaven and on earth and under the earth and on the sea, and all that is in them singing: 'To him who sits on the throne and to the Lamb be praise and honor and glory and power, for ever and ever!'"

The theme song of heaven is focused on the greatness of God and all He has done and continues to do. He is so magnificent, beautiful, and awe-inspiring that every type of creature and personality who sees Him cannot help but to worship, thank, and honor Him. I think it is a little bit like seeing the sunset on a beach with a huge ocean in front of

Section I—The Platform

you, or seeing a snow-capped range of mountains or a crystal-clear mountain lake, or taking in the stars on a clear night, and being in awe of what is before you. You cannot help but to be taken in; to stay focused on its wonder. That is how it is in heaven with beings that actually get to see God. As the classic hit song by Frankie Valli goes, "You're just too good to be true. I can't take my eyes off of you." When you see God as He really is, songs of adoration and expression just have to be sung. In the last couple of chapters, we talked about realizations or revelations, and how these lead to liberation; this is especially true in seeing what God is like. The more we see Him and realize what His true nature is, the more we fall in love with Him, the more we want to worship and adore Him, and then live from Him and for Him.

The song of our world, on the other hand, goes something like this: "I am the center of the universe. It really is all about me. Meet my needs. I need to be fulfilled. I need love. I am the one my world revolves around." As much as we hate to admit it, this is the song that drives the world apart from God. All of us, at our core, are naturally selfish. We come into the world that way. Little babies look so sweet and innocent, and they are, but a baby is only concerned about its needs and wants. They have absolutely no problem with crying at the top of their lungs in the middle of the night when everyone is sleeping, or right in the middle of an important meeting. "I need something and I need it right now!" is how they respond. Little children can be incredibly kind and loving, but if you have ever been to a playground, it is not generally a place of friendly sharing where each little angel kindly offers to share his toys with playmates. Very often, it is more like a little war zone with attitudes and actions like, "I want that toy. If I'm bigger

Chapter 5 • Changing Your Theme Song

and stronger than you, I'm going to take it." I'll never forget when our oldest son was around two years old and we took him to the playground behind our apartment for the first time. He went out there all excited to play with some new friends. The first kid he met gave him a martial arts-type nerve pinch around his neck and tried to take his toy. Where does a four year old learn to do that? Welcome to the world, son. As we get older, we learn to control it more and hide it better, but at our core, we sing the song of the world system, "I am worthy." That is the dominating spirit or soul condition of unredeemed man. That is our theme song before receiving Christ.

If we want to partner with the greatest person in the universe, our song needs to be in harmony with the rest of God's choir. They are living in perfect agreement with God, and His power and presence are assuring His perfect will is being done in that realm, in heaven. When we make the song of heaven our theme song, it helps us order our lives with the order God has set up. It gets to the heart of things, helps us focus correctly, and brings great power and release. Everyone who makes the shift and makes the song of heaven their theme song, experiences life in a whole new way.

When we stop singing, "It is all about me," and instead start singing, "You are worthy, God," we invite God the King to rule in our lives and circumstances. Psalm 22:3 tells us "God inhabits (or sets up His throne in) our praises." He will not shove His way into our hearts, but if we invite Him to be our king, "He will come in power and love." In his famous booklet, *The Four Spiritual Laws*, Bill Bright put it well when he instructed, "I must step down from the throne of my life and let God take His rightful place there." Only one person can sit on that throne at a

Section I–The Platform

time and since He is God, He is the Creator of the universe; He is the only one worthy to rule my life. This is a tough decision for all of us, because the temptation from the very beginning has been: "I want to be like God, knowing good from evil. I want to be the boss" (Genesis 3). God never takes our ability to choose away from us. Even when we sing the song of heaven, we still cast the deciding vote on our decisions. However, if we want to move in God's flow, we must go to the cross, submit our lives totally to His leadership, and live His way. Jesus said it like this, "If any of you wants to be my follower, you must put aside your selfish ambition, shoulder your cross daily, and follow me. If you try to keep your life for yourself, you will lose it. But if you give up your life for me, you will find true life" (Luke 9:23–24 NLT).

It sounds like a bummer to give up what you want and make what God wants your focus, but it is a divine paradox. When you live for yourself, the happiness you experience is short-lived. When you continually sing the song of heaven and put Jesus first (His will, plans, and purposes), then comes a release of life from God's Spirit to you. People who are totally self-absorbed, living for them and theirs, are, in the long run, miserable and messed up people. When you live for "me," happiness is short-lived because it is against God's order of life. When you pick up your cross and put what God wants first, there is a level of joy and peace that you, otherwise, would never have.

Why does it need to be that way? God designed us to live with Him as our center and source. We will look at this more in the next chapter, but let me introduce it here. God designed us to live with Him as our core focus. Many people do not experience His love and grace because they have Him simply as a part, a compartment, in their lives. They

Chapter 5 • Changing Your Theme Song

divide up their lives into nice little sections: family, work, recreation, self-improvement, and God. Living that way, though, is like trying to drive with no air in your tires. You can have these four tires of life, each one important, and each one made with great potential to help you go far. It is possible to drive for a while with no air in your tires, but it will be a rough ride and will eventually ruin your car, leaving you stuck in life. God needs to be like the air in the tires. Not just in one or two of them, but in all of them. He wants to be involved in every area of our lives so He can fill every area, or every tire if you will, with His lifting presence. In order to do that, you must fill your tires first, not fill them somewhere down the road. God needs to be first, involved in every area of our lives, to progress on the journey and arrive at our final destination.

When I came to Christ as a freshman in college, I prayed in my dorm room one night and asked Jesus into my life. I basically said, "God, I know I have screwed up real bad. You have every reason to send me to hell. But, You said that Jesus died for my sins, all of them, and that You would take me back if I come to You. Lord, please forgive me and take me back as I now receive Jesus as my Lord and Savior." Immediately, a weight was lifted off my soul, a peace came in my heart, a joy sprang up, and the realization that God truly was my Father. It was a wonderful, life-changing night I will never forget, but the peace, joy, and realization of God's love did not stick with me. I was not experiencing ongoing fruitfulness.

I talked it over with a friend who had been a Christ-follower a couple of years longer than me. He asked me if I had made Jesus the Lord of my life. He then explained to me that Jesus needed to have first place in my life and become my focus and source if I wanted to have lasting life.

Section I—The Platform

He showed me the passage from Luke 9 that you read just a few moments ago. I saw it and I got it. Even though I had received Jesus' forgiveness and the new life He offered, I had not made Him my #1. So, I prayed and said, "Jesus, I want you to take first place in my life. Be my Lord (or my leader). I want to pick up my cross and do it your way." From that time on, a new level of life was released in me. It does the same for every person who makes that step.

This is an absolutely crucial step, and one that God has emphasized over and over again. In Exodus 12 and 13, God had just struck the final blow to the false gods of Egypt by striking down the first born of all the Egyptians. Just as the Israelites are leaving Egypt, God instructs Moses to tell the people of Israel to make sure they celebrate Passover (a picture of salvation) every year from this time on. The next thing He addresses is the consecration, or dedication, of the people of Israel's first born to Him. Whether the first-born son, the first-born of their cattle, or the first fruits of the crops they would harvest, God said, "the first belongs to Me." Before they are even completely out of Egypt, before they have crossed the Red Sea (a picture of baptism), God says you need to make this shift, you need to sing this song. God needs to be first place in every area, all the time.

God does not give us this requirement because He is selfish and insecure; He is doing just great, thank you. He gives us this commandment to help us, and those around us. Jesus said, "Seek first the kingdom of God and His righteousness," then, "all these things will be added to you" (Matthew 6:33). The order is crucial. If we seek Him first, everything else we need will be given to us at the right time. If we change that order, putting anything else in front of God, it all gets screwed up. It could be called the typewriter or keyboard principle. Right now, I am sitting at my

Chapter 5 • Changing Your Theme Song

computer, typing out words that everyone who understands English can at least read. However, if my fingers move over to the right or left, up or down, just one key, then what I type would come out on the screen and page as gibberish. Despite my own understanding of what I am trying to communicate, giving it my best effort, if my fingers do not line up correctly on the keyboard, it does not work right. My fingers have to line up on the right keys from the start for this process to work. If I want to live the way God designed me to, I need to line my life up the way He says, with Jesus first in my life.

I have seen it repeatedly through the years. Like me, many have an initial "new life in Christ" experience when they receive Jesus as their Savior, but for that life to continue and increase, this bridge must be crossed, and the sooner the better. Jesus said that it is a tough decision and we should take some time and carefully consider it or "count the cost," but make no mistake about it, with the regular pressures we all face from the world we live in to go in a wrong direction, this step must be taken. Jesus must take over first place and become more important to us than anything else. When He does assume that position, the price we pay is dwarfed by the rewards that come.

Jesus said, "What does it profit a person to gain the whole world and lose his soul?" (Luke 9:25). So what if you have a great home, a lot of money, power, fame, or pleasure for a few years. It is gone quickly and then we face eternity (a never-ending dimension). Motivational speaker Peter Lowe uses the following illustration when talking to crowds about this theme: "If I could make you a millionaire overnight, would you like that?" Of course, everyone says yes. Lowe then says, "What if you could be a millionaire, but only for a day, would you like that?" Peo-

Section I—The Platform

ple respond, "No. That would not be good." Lowe then says, "That is what it is like to gain great success in this world without having God #1 in your life. It is all here for a short time and then you spend forever with nothing." It is obvious what the right choice should be—put Jesus first.

Yet I have seen many people through the years get ripped off by not seeing the big picture, focusing instead on that one thing they just have to have. Once they have it, then they have to have the next "one thing," and then the next one. If a person would just step back for a moment and look at where this is leading them, they would soon recognize it is the devil's strategy to take them away from God's way of life. The "I just need this next one thing" journey always ends in a wasted and disappointing life. Real joy and happiness are found only by refusing to let anything else take God's rightful place and by putting and keeping Jesus first.

Jesus was not misleading us when He said that if we lose our life for His sake, then we will find it. He experienced it Himself when He said yes to God and no to His own desire and went to the cross for us. He did suffer, but then God raised Him up and exalted Him above every other name and power in every dimension forever. The same principle applies to us; when we give up our lives for God, He loves to bless us in abundance.

God will not take your will away from you. He will not make you His robot or puppet. He makes you His son or daughter and invites you to walk with Him, fellowship with Him, and work with Him in important endeavors. However, there can only be one boss, one head, one senior partner, and it has to be God.

Chapter 5 • Changing Your Theme Song

Will you exchange your theme song? Instead of singing that old, worn out "It's all about me" song, will you begin singing the song of heaven?

"You are worthy, O Lord our God, to receive glory and honor and power. For you created everything, and it is for your pleasure that they exist and were created" (Revelation 4:10-11 NLT).

Section II—The Power

Chapter I
Jesus the Life Changer

    Shortly after starting a church in Munich, Germany, a few of us went for a day's outing to Neuschwanstein Castle (the castle that Disneyland® and Walt Disney World® used as a model). The other American couple we worked with did not yet have a car, so they borrowed a good-looking Mercedes from a new church member. We saw beautiful scenery as we drove through the foothills of the Bavarian Alps, and we enjoyed the day at King Ludwig's impressive castle. It was late afternoon when we started on our trip back to Munich. We were all low on fuel, so we pulled into a gas station to fill up. My friend, never having driven a Mercedes before, filled up the tank with diesel fuel and we headed down the road. That would have been just fine had the car had a diesel engine. However, it did not. Because of my friend's limited knowledge of Mercedes automobiles, he assumed they all ran on diesel fuel, when in fact, the ma-

Section II—The Power

jority do not. My wife, Janet, and I were driving behind them so we had a first hand look at what happened next. After just a few minutes, the Mercedes started belching out black plumes of smoke. The wonderful driving machine began shaking and sputtering, acting more like an old jalopy rather than the exceptional car it was. From our vantage point, it looked hilarious, like a scene from a comedy—clunking, sputtering, and spitting down the road as the car left a trail of black smoke behind it. It was a really a funny sight and one that is still clear in my mind over twenty years later. Of course, I was not driving the Mercedes, and for my friend and their guests, it wasn't very funny at all. They had to drive over two hours back to Munich in this condition, until the car had burned up the diesel fuel and they could put in the right kind of fuel. On top of that, they had to explain to the new church member what had happened to his car. I am sure the owner of the car wondered what types of people were leading the new church he had joined. Amazingly, he stayed with us for some time after that.

That Mercedes was a quality machine through and through. However wonderfully designed, it would only function well when used as intended and given the right fuel. The Bible tells us we also are fearfully and wonderfully made (Psalm 139), a God creation. We only function well, however, when we operate according to the maker's instructions. We were designed by God to live with Him as our center, our focus, and our source. Jesus could not have said it any clearer, "Remain in me, and I will remain in you. For a branch cannot produce fruit if it is severed from the vine, and you cannot be fruitful apart from me. Yes, I am the vine; you are the branches. Those who remain in

Chapter I • Jesus the Life Changer

me, and I in them, will produce much fruit. For apart from me, you can do nothing" (John 15:4-5 NLT).

Sometimes Christians think that the only reason Jesus came was to get us into heaven. Securing our eternity and making sure we get into heaven is certainly a major reason Jesus came, and in the light of eternity, the most important benefit of salvation. Nevertheless, Jesus said He also came to give us abundant, fruitful, loving, joy-filled, peace guided lives now in this world. The person, Jesus Christ, is not just a concept, but the most important key to real life and real life change. Jesus, the person, came into this world and engaged it. He spoke, took action, touched people, and touched the world. In only a few short years, Jesus changed the world and continues to change it even centuries later. Jesus is not only a world changer, but He is an individual life changer as well.

When Jesus began His public ministry, He set in motion a tidal wave force that forever changed the heavenly and the earthly realms. As soon as He was baptized in water and filled with the Holy Spirit, He was led by God into the wilderness to face the god of this world, Satan, for forty days. Satan hit him with his best shots, but Jesus soundly defeated him and came to the public in the power of the Holy Spirit, prepared to change lives. It is clear from Scripture there was a whole lot going on here on planet earth that God did not like, and at the right time, He entered the world as a man to do something about it. Matthew 4:16–17 (NIV) says, "the people living in darkness have seen a great light; and to them which sat in the region and shadow of death light is sprung up." The world was in spiritual darkness, and the death process ruled until Jesus came. When Jesus came on the scene, the world began to change as never before. This Isaiah-prophesied sermon came to life in Galilee

Section II—The Power

the moment Jesus started preaching. He picked up where John left off. "Change your life. God's kingdom is here" (Matthew 4:17 The Message).

In essence, Jesus told these well-designed but wrongly connected and fueled people, "I've come to change things; to change your lives, to open up a whole dimension to you where God is your source, your focus, and your center. Entirely new things are now possible and available for each person who will enter into God's kingdom and let God enter them." He then began going everywhere teaching, preaching, healing the sick, setting free the oppressed, and introducing people to life the way God intended it to be.

He taught them that God did not want them living in darkness, fear, and oppression. 1 John 3:8 (NASB) states that "The Son of God appeared for this purpose, to destroy the works of the devil," and Acts 10:38 (NASB) says, "You know of Jesus of Nazareth, how God anointed Him with the Holy Spirit and power, and how He went about doing good and healing all who were oppressed by the devil, for God was with Him."

For change to happen in our lives, this understanding is huge! We need to see that Jesus really does want to change our lives for the good. Not everything happening on this planet is His Will; in fact, a lot of it is the total opposite of what He desires for us.

Several years ago, there was a young wife and mother who attended a church we served; we'll call her Sally. Sally had a long history of debilitating fear that had caused her to attempt suicide, run away from her family, hide from loved ones, and, in general, had made her life miserable. Several times over the years, I visited her in the psych ward of a local hospital. She had prayed to God to set her free from this fear, but it did not go away. She went to Christian

Chapter I • Jesus the Life Changer

counseling, yet it still did not get better. She took medication and that did not work either. She then started hanging out with a sincere Christian woman who had had severe emotional and health problems for years. She tried to comfort Sally and tell her God was doing this to her to work something into her life, so she should just accept it and yield to it. I know that God does use suffering, and there are problems that do not go away in this lifetime, but there are many issues that God *does* want to deal with here and now. He uses many different means, such as prayer, worship, good teaching, counseling, and medication, but far too many people assume that God does not want to change the situation because it does not happen immediately.

Janet and I began to tell her that based on Scripture, God did not want her dominated and incapacitated by fear. This paralyzing, life-robbing fear was part of the darkness that Jesus came to drive away. There are hundreds of Scriptures like 2 Timothy 1:7, that tell us God does not want us to fear. Eventually, Sally began listening to us and resisting the fear, in the name of Jesus. She began using Scripture as a sword, worship as a weapon, and got positive Christian support. She drew on the strength and power that Jesus has to change lives and, gradually, she began to come out of it. Day by day, week by week, the times of fear began to lessen. Over time, her whole life and her family's lives all changed because of it. More than ten years have passed, and now, she is a beautiful Christian woman with a great family, a servant's heart, who is touching lives through her ministry. That is the power of the person, Jesus Christ, and realizing that Jesus came to change things.

Presently, if you visit any bookstore, you will find a large section of self-help books. Some are based on eastern religions; others simply offer practical steps that people can

Section II—The Power

take to modify behaviors. These books always have testimonies of people who tell how these steps or practices helped them change. Some are impressive and I do not think all of them are exaggerated or fraudulent. There are truths and helpful steps found in all types of philosophies and beliefs. Yet, no matter how spectacular the stories, they are still very limited in their depth. Any help that does not have Jesus as its center is going to fall short, or be incomplete, because we were designed to live with Him as our source, or to use Jesus' words, "our vine." For lasting change to happen, only Jesus can get to the core issues.

Many popular philosophies of today tell us that God is already in us, or a life force we can call *God* is inside each and every one of us. They may say that it does not matter what you call it, that you just need to recognize it and learn the steps to release it. Nevertheless, this just does not work; at least in fullness or completeness. As Rick Warren wrote in *The Purpose Driven Life*,

"...you won't discover life's meaning by looking within yourself. You've probably tried that already. You didn't create yourself, so there is no way you can tell yourself what you were created for! If I handed you an invention you had never seen before, you wouldn't know its purpose, and the invention itself wouldn't be able to tell you either. Only the creator or the owner's manual could reveal its purpose" (Warren 2002, 18).

What is true of finding our purpose is also true of living it. We are not self-sufficient beings; we are dependent on outside sources for physical life. We must have food, water, and air to survive. Once ingested, these give us strength, but without them, we would soon perish. The spiritual is similar. We can only see some growth and change happen on the limited resources we have in ourselves. These may

Chapter I • Jesus the Life Changer

seem significant compared to people who are nourishing their inner life on nothing but sitcoms or MTV, but it is still so small compared to what happens to people who invite the Creator of the universe into their life.

According to Jesus' closest follower, John, Jesus did so many miracles that if all of them were recorded, all the books in the world could not contain them (John 20). Remember that Jesus:

- Healed every type of sickness and illness imaginable—physical, mental, emotional, and social—in scores of people. Sometimes crowds of thousands were healed at one service.
- Multiplied limited resources.
- Relieved people of guilt, shame, and hopelessness.
- Turned average people into world changers.
- Gave the very wisdom of God on how to live well.
- Raised the dead and was raised from the dead Himself.

This is who we are looking to for power and wisdom to change. We are not looking to our own limited strength and resources. We are looking to the source and sustainer of life itself. If I had to pick one key on living life well (which I don't, because God has many for us), but if I did, it would be this: Jesus Christ is the life. Jesus Christ is my life. He is the beginning and the end of all things. He is the author and finisher of my faith. He is at work in me to work out His will and His pleasure in me. He has committed Himself to completing the good work He has started in me. He is the way, the truth, and the life. He is the Creator of the universe. He is the One who holds all things together by His powerful words. He is the resurrection and the light of the

Section II—The Power

world, and in Him are hidden all treasures of wisdom and knowledge. All these New Testament phrases tell us it really is a relationship with the Savior, not a formula, which produces real life.

That is why the most important thing we can do is to develop a close, intimate relationship with Him. He is at work in us as a master craftsman. He knows exactly what blessings and challenges we need to grow into His image and He knows the order in which we need them. In the Exodus, the children of Israel followed a cloud by day and a pillar of fire by night. If this presence of God stayed one day in a place, they stayed one day. If it stayed for a year, they stayed a year. This is a picture of how we are to follow Jesus in our life's journey. Some things He moves us through quickly, others take some time, but if we stay close enough to hear His still, small voice in our hearts, He will give us the grace we need to change and grow according to what He is working on at that time.

I wish that when I came to Christ, God made me perfect right then. To be honest, I wish He had made you perfect too because you and I both mess it up far too often for my liking. But He doesn't do that. Why not? In Exodus 23:29-30 (NASB) God told Israel, "I will not drive them (enemies) out before you in a single year, that the land may not become desolate and the beasts of the field become too numerous for you. I will drive them out before you little by little, until you become fruitful and take possession of the land." God told them that even though the Promised Land was theirs for the taking, they would not conquer it overnight. It would not even be done in a year. It would take years to posses their entire promised future. It is not enough to drive out an enemy; we need to be able to take possession of it and be able to live in it as well. When we become

Chapter 1 • Jesus the Life Changer

fruitful enough (the result of walking closely with Jesus and partnering with Him), then we take possession of that future. We do not just taste it every now and then; it is something we regularly experience.

I have noticed in my own life and the lives of others, that we sometimes experience a breakthrough in a particular area for a time, but often slip back, lose it, or are unable to sustain it. We have taken new land, but have not yet reached a level of maturity and stability to be able to maintain it and live in it as a lifestyle. In weight lifting competitions, the lifter has to hold the weight until the judge says he has control of it. It is not enough to get it to the lift position and immediately drop it; the weight must be controlled and held for a period of time in order to be counted. The same is true of spiritual and life progress. God does not want us just to experience life one time, or on occasion, He wants us to *live* in the Promised Land.

In John 10, Jesus described His interaction with us as a shepherd. Shepherds of that era would keep the sheep in a safe area during the evenings, and then lead them out into pasture during the day. As the shepherd took the sheep to new pasturelands, he would often move their pen as well, still using this "out during the day and back in at night" routine. As we follow closely after Jesus, He leads us out into new areas of pasture (or blessing) where we experience new aspects of His life for a time. Because these new pastures often stretch us and take us out of the known or comfortable, He then takes us back into the secure and known for a while. He knows we are not yet strong enough to be able to hold it, to possess it, so he repeats this process, leading us out and back in, until eventually He sees we are able to sustain it. He then moves the whole operation as we progressively learn to live on new ground. The once new areas

Section II—The Power

become the daily experience until He leads us out to new pastures again at the right time. No wonder the most famous of Psalms describes the Lord as our Shepherd leading us to green meadows and peaceful streams, as well as through the dark valleys and feasts in the presence of our enemies (Psalm 23). Jesus uses all of these experiences as only He can.

Let me illustrate from my own life. As I stated earlier, I am naturally somewhat of a skeptic and critic. I am not always this way, but it definitely surfaces enough that I count it as one of my negative traits. It is not something I'm proud of; nevertheless, without Jesus I can find the problem in just about any situation. Over the years, I have gradually improved, gotten more positive, encouraging, and joyful, but I still slip back into that negative spirit from time to time. Jesus has led, and continues to lead, me into new experiences and insights of being positive and joyful. Although I love being more positive, because I still deal with that old nature, I do not always "hold" that joy or "possess" that promise. So, Jesus lets me rest a little, leading me into circumstances where I do not have to put forth much, if any, effort to be positive and joyful. Then He says, "Okay, let's face some challenges where you have to learn to let My joy and faith flow through you. Let's take some new ground and hold it a little longer." Jesus, my source and my shepherd, my leader and personal trainer, is working in me like no one or nothing else can. Every year the negativity is less, and I grow in faith and joy, and have a more positive outlook on life. I may never be perfect in those areas in this lifetime, but I am much better than I used to be. When I speak at church or in other settings, the comment I hear most often from those who heard me is, "That was so encouraging. That really gave me hope and strengthened my

Chapter I • Jesus the Life Changer

faith." That is Jesus at work; taking a skeptic and making him into an instrument of faith, hope, and love is God at work. He has done, and continues to do, something I could never have done on my own. I am growing, changing, and taking possession of the promised future God has for me, but it does not happen overnight.

When we make Jesus our life, we do not have to live like the rest of the world. We are not dependent on external circumstances. There is a life available in Him that is greater than anything the world knows or the challenges life throws at us. Our Savior, the Creator, is at work in us to drive out the works of the enemy and to bring us into the future He desires us to have.

If your desire is to please Him, then never think He gets tired of working with you. He absolutely loves doing these awesome works of restoration in your life and in mine. He is patient, wise, and understands exactly what is going on in our lives and what it will take to get us into the Promised Land of His desired future for us. Jesus is the Way, He is the Truth, and He is the Life, so get to know Him well through Bible reading, prayer, and the other spiritual pathways He has made available to us.

Chapter 2
Rut-Busting Holy Spirit Power

Webster's Ninth New Collegiate Dictionary defines a rut as "a track worn by a wheel or by habitual passage; a groove in which something runs; a usual or fixed practice: a monotonous routine." Some have said that a rut is a grave with the ends kicked out. A rut, of course, does not start out as one. At first, it is simply one of many options, but as that same route is followed repeatedly, over time, it gradually wears out the existing path and a deeper groove develops. The more often this path is followed, the deeper the rut becomes and the more difficult it is to go any other way. If you have ever ridden a bicycle on trails, you know how much effort it takes to get out of a rut once you have gotten into one. We all have "ruts" in our souls that have become a way of life for us. They are generally not intentional; they just develop as we go about life. If we stay in these soul ruts, life becomes bland and boring at best, and crippling

Chapter 2 • Rut-Busting Holy Spirit Power

and destructive at worst. I do not know of anyone who wants to live in a rut, yet it happens repeatedly. Thankfully, God has provided a way out. First, it is helpful to realize what some of the main ruts are and then how to draw on God's strength to get out them.

One of the most monotonous, rut-like voices in the minds of many sincere Christ followers sounds like this: "If you really loved God and people you would not be doing things like that. You are a hypocrite. You are not sincere. You are a disgrace to the cause of Christ, and not only that; you must really like that sin otherwise you would not do it!" When received, we not only have to deal with the consequences of our mistakes, we then also have to deal with the black cloud of despair and hopelessness these thoughts produce. This rut can easily make us feel like we are in a grave, with the ends still firmly in place!

The problem is that there is truth to those statements. When I do not practice what I preach, I really could be a two-faced hypocrite. Jesus was so gracious to people who realized they needed God's help, but He was tough with religious hypocrites. Hypocrites in the church are one of the main excuses unchurched people give for not going. "What an awful person I must be, saying one thing, but having trouble living it. Jesus must not like me and people are going to hell because of my lousy, weak lifestyle."

On top of that, if I really do love God and people, how can I keep doing things I know displease or hurt them? To be honest, some of my sins do have a degree of pleasure to them; unhealthy food can taste so good, overpowering someone can make me feel so strong and superior. I must really want to do them. I must be rotten on the inside; otherwise I would not want to do these things. Maybe I really do not want to live a holy, God-pleasing life. After all, in

Section II—The Power

my entire life I never succumb to the temptation of eating Brussels sprouts. Brussels sprouts could use their greatest powers of persuasion and seduction, they could call to me with a sexy voice, they could cover themselves in chocolate, they could offer me the world, yet I would never give in to them. I tried eating them once as a kid and almost threw up right at the table. As an adult, trying to eat a healthy diet, I tried again with the same result. I hate brussel sprouts; therefore, they are never a temptation to me. But some of these sins, I keep on doing."

It is ironic that this is a problem mainly for sincere believers. The very people who most want to live a God-pleasing life deal with internal, and sometimes external, accusations of not being sincere. On the other hand, people who do not really care about living a God-pleasing life often just shrug it off, rationalize it, or shift the blame to someone else. Because sincere Christians often realize their own sins and failures, it is very possible to live under a cloud of guilt and despair.

When faced with difficulties it does help to know that others have gone through the same things that we have. If we think we are the only one facing a particular problem or the only one having trouble getting past it, we can feel even worse than just having to deal with the problem itself. The rise of support and recovery groups has helped us see the power of being open and honest about our struggles, and getting comfort and support from others who are facing the same things we do. This is one of the ways the Bible is so helpful; it is brutally honest about the failures and challenges people have faced, as well as the answers they received. It does not just tell us about the wonderful people and the victorious times in their lives, it also gives the ugly details of people's failures.

Chapter 2 • Rut-Busting Holy Spirit Power

Aside from Jesus Himself, probably no other Christian in the history of the world has had as powerful an impact as the Apostle Paul. Used by God to plant churches in areas totally unfamiliar with the Christian message, he saw the words he taught confirmed over and over again with great miracles performed by God. He wrote a large portion of the New Testament with insights that He received directly from God, Himself, regarding the uniqueness and greatness of Christ and the amazing riches that God has provided for us. He was a man "on fire" for God, a world changer, willing to sacrifice his life to fulfill his calling; yet, he too, understood and battled some of the same things we do. Look at how he describes it in Romans 7:15, 18, and 24 (NLT), "I don't understand myself at all, for I really want to do what is right, but I don't do it. Instead I do the very thing I hate …I know I am rotten through and through so far as my old sinful nature is concerned. No matter which way I turn, I can't make myself do right. I want to, but I can't. When I want to do good, I don't. And when I try not to do wrong, I do it anyway …Oh, what a miserable person I am! Who will free me from this life that is dominated by sin?"

This is both comforting and insightful. It helps to know that even Paul, the super apostle and world changer, understood what it is like to do things he did not want to do. He too said he wanted to do right but ended up doing wrong. This lets us know it does not necessarily mean we are insincere or do not love God if we struggle with repeated sins. It does mean that even in a born again believer, we live in bodies that are drawn to sin and have areas of our souls that still need renewing and renovation. In Galatians 5, Paul wrote that the Spirit and the sin nature are in opposition to one another. That tells me that at my core, I can really desire to do right, but can have trouble doing it be-

Section II—The Power

cause of the power of sin at work in other areas of my soul. I'm not an uncaring hypocrite, I'm not deluding myself into thinking I want to please God when I really don't, rather, there is a struggle taking place that even the greatest saints experienced. That is comforting.

However, if we think it through, it can also be discouraging. Are we never going to be able to defeat these sins? Are we doomed to live the rest of our lives under the domination of these death producing thoughts, words, and actions? No wonder Paul wrote about how miserable this was. Throughout history, those who understood this, including the great reformer Martin Luther, did experience internal torment. Luther experienced great anguish when he realized how holy and good God was, and how sin had stained every level of his soul, with no way out. For Paul, Luther, and all of us, if we do not get some help it becomes an agonizing way to live rather than the overflowing life Jesus talked about.

Thankfully, Paul does not just write about the problem, he also gives us the God solutions in the next passages. We're going to break it down with five S's; two of which are shown below, and the remaining shown in chapter three.

1. Put on God's **Suit**

"Therefore, there is now no condemnation for those who are *in Christ Jesus*, because through Christ Jesus the law of the Spirit of life set me free from the law of sin and death" (Rom. 8:1–2 NIV).

No person, aside from Jesus, has ever batted a thousand in life. Each one of us has sinned countless times and can never repay that debt. The gospel of God is that Jesus did for us what we could never do. He lived a sinless life, then

Chapter 2 • Rut-Busting Holy Spirit Power

took all of our sin on Himself on the cross, paying that debt in full. Three days later, God raised Him from the dead and now offers forgiveness, cleansing, and eternal life as a gift to everyone who will receive Him.

Recently, there was a television commercial for a video game in which a superstar of the National Basketball Association (NBA) is doing amazing basketball feats on the court. He then walks off the court and, to the viewer's surprise, he robotically opens up and a normal looking man steps out of the superstar's figure. This average, normal looking man then walks over to another superstar figure, opens him up, steps inside, and begins playing in his "suit." In a way, this is what happens to us when we receive Jesus. Spiritually speaking, God clothes us with Christ, with His perfect righteousness, so that we are completely covered before God; we are "in Christ." No one could tell the normal looking fellow was in the superstar suit until he opened it up and stepped out. As long as we trust Jesus for our salvation, we are in Christ's suit. That is why the Bible encourages us to come to God with boldness and confidence. We are not dependent on our own purity, rightness or efforts, but on the perfect holiness of Jesus Himself. Jesus is God's answer for the problems of sin, for the guilt and despair that try to torment us. When we are faced with our sinful shortcomings, we do not hide them or rationalize them, we bring them to God, ask His forgiveness, get back up, and keep on living in the covering of Jesus. The Bible is extremely bold on this point. It says there is actually no, zero, zilch condemnation for those in Christ. Because God does not condemn the Son, He does not condemn us. The Message translation of Romans 8:2 says it this way, "The Spirit of life in Christ, like a strong wind, has magnificently cleared the air, freeing you from a fated lifetime of brutal tyranny at the hands of sin and death." We do not have to listen to those "in the rut" voices of accusation any longer. If we are in Christ, we are free from the brutal tyranny of sin and Satan's tormenting words.

2. Live in the Power of God's Spirit

"The Spirit of life set me free ...You, however, are controlled not by the sinful nature but by the Spirit, if *the Spirit of God lives in you* ...And if the *Spirit* of him who raised Jesus from the dead *is living in you*, he who raised Jesus from the dead will also give life to your mortal bodies through His Spirit who lives in you" (Romans 8:1, 9, 11 NIV). God not only clothes us with Christ, He also puts His very own Holy Spirit inside us. Three times in these few short verses, God says the Holy Spirit lives inside those who have received Jesus. I do not know how God does it, but He Himself moves into our inner man by His Spirit and the Holy Spirit has the power to do what we could never do in our own strength.

Of all the descriptions in the Bible used elsewhere that Paul could have used here to describe the Holy Spirit's work in us (fruit, water, fire, wind, etc.), he chooses to use the greatest miracle of all time, the resurrection of Jesus. Years ago, I heard a great illustration to help people see that they could never be good enough in their own abilities to get into heaven. It goes like this: when we realize that any thought, word, or action that is contrary to God's nature and word is sin, if we are honest, we must admit we all sin a lot. For the sake of illustration, let's imagine a near perfect person who only sins three times in a day. That person only has one bad thought, one wrong word, and one wrong action in an entire day. If we add up those three sins a day, over the course of one year, it adds up to over one

Chapter 2 • Rut-Busting Holy Spirit Power

thousand sins. Multiply that by the average lifespan today (approximately seventy-seven years) and, for a near perfect person, they come to God with seventy-seven thousand sins. That is a truly ridiculous amount for anyone claiming to be a "good person." How would that add up for the rest of us? When we realize, according to God, that just one sin produces death, we see how it is impossible for anyone to be good enough to make it to heaven through their own efforts. That is why we need the Savior, Jesus.

As I thought about this in relation to Jesus on the cross, it hit me how overwhelming a burden Jesus bore. Imagine the sins of not just one person, with hundreds of thousands of them in their account, but of the billions of people who have ever lived or ever will; billions of people with hundreds of thousands of sins each. All of that was poured onto Jesus on the cross. Theologians have rightly said, "Only God could die for the sins of an entire world." In my mind, I saw it like a huge building imploding, with each brick being a sin and each building being an individual life. Imagine billions of buildings, uncountable tons of material, come crashing down …all of it on the Son of God. He was, in a very real sense, buried under the sin of the world.

Yet, three days later, the Spirit of God raised Jesus up from this unimaginable weight. The Apostle Peter declared it was impossible for death to hold Him. In the spiritual dimension, maybe it was like a rocket taking off with such power that He blasted Satan's power structure into little pieces, even as God set Him at His right hand, far above all power and authority and dominion (Eph. 1:20–22). Paul wrote that this is the Spirit who now lives in each and every believer. The same Spirit that raised Jesus from the dead now lives in us. Death was sin's most powerful consequence, its most awful power. If the Holy Spirit can per-

Section II—The Power

form that type of miracle in Jesus, raising Him from the unimaginable weight of all those skyscrapers of sin, what can He do with the power of sin that comes against you? Compared to what He's already done, it's just a few bricks that need to be moved. True, they may be deeply lodged in your soul, perhaps even part of the foundation of who you are, yet you need to realize that it does not matter how long you have struggled with a sin or weakness. It does not matter how long it has been in your family or how strong a hold it has had in your life. It is tiny compared to the power of the Holy Spirit within you. Resurrection power is in you and me, right now, through the Holy Spirit, and Jesus said this wonderful Holy Spirit is here to help us.

One of the toughest problems people face today, especially men, is in the area of pornography. These images can lodge themselves in a person's mind for years, and if a man or woman starts watching these easily accessible sites and channels, it can quickly become an addiction. I am so proud of a group of men at our church, and at other churches around the country, who are not rationalizing their addiction, not denying it, not hiding it, and not giving up. Rather, they are drawing together in small groups to open up their lives, support one another, and draw on God's resurrection power to break this addiction and walk in purity. As I talk with these men, I hear their stories of real headway and progress. Some chains of the soul like this one are not easily broken, but these men have hope because they are dependent on God's Spirit, not their own strength, to help them walk free of this problem. They are marching onward and upward and it is wonderful to see the hope and light in their eyes as they are gaining victory. God's Spirit will work in all of us too.

Chapter 2 • Rut-Busting Holy Spirit Power

Because the Holy Spirit is invisible to our natural eyes and because we do not always feel Him in our emotions (often we do, but not always), it is relatively easy to be unaware of Him and *not* draw on His strength. Spiritual realities are not always emotional realities. Nevertheless, He is always present with us, and available to us, whether we are having a powerful feeling right then or not. Romans 8:26 tells us He knows the mind of God, He knows what God is doing, and what God is working on at every phase of our lives. As we train ourselves to be aware of Him and learn to be led by Him, His power will be present to do what God wants done at every step of our journey. It is a journey out of the rut and into the freedom of Jesus.

Chapter 3
The Mind and the Holy Spirit

    I first started in vocational ministry in a campus setting. At the time, several of the leaders in our ministry were telling everyone how they were following John Wesley's model of getting up at 4:00 a.m. to pray, study, and be spiritually ready for a day of ministry. John Wesley was a man used by God to change his nation and many others through the Methodist movement. I also heard others tell of how Wesley used to break his day up into ten-minute increments to make sure he made maximum use of his time. Hearing all this as a young impressionable minister, I decided to follow Wesley's, and these other leaders', example. I started getting up at 4:00 a.m. and made schedules of every minute of the day so I would maximize each day for God. Like so many good ideas, it worked well for a couple of weeks. I was having rich prayer and study times, undisturbed by anyone in those special early morning hours.

Chapter 3 • The Mind and the Holy Spirit

Then real life set in. I was so tired that I was falling asleep any time I sat still for more than a couple of minutes throughout the day. I was driving my wife crazy, constantly asking her opinion on how I could best schedule every minute, because every time I set up the "perfect" schedule, someone or something would mess it up. (I know this sounds insane to some of you, probably most of you, but I really wanted to give God my best and this was the model I was trying to follow.) I finally came to my senses one night when I got a phone call. I stumbled to the phone (we lived in married student housing, with just one phone on the wall) and mumbled "Hello" into the receiver. A minister friend was on the other end and he said, "Mark, sorry to call so late, but I needed to let you know about something."

I said, "That's okay, I was about to get up anyway."

He started laughing and said, "What time do you think it is?"

"Close to four," I replied.

"No, it's midnight. What kind of insane schedule are you on? You don't know if it's day or night."

Right then I decided I just could not keep up with John Wesley or with these other ministers either. It was hard because I wanted to measure up, I wanted to make the most of my life, and here at the very beginning of my ministry, I saw that I could not hold to their standards. Shortly thereafter, I got some additional key information. I found out that Wesley went to bed at 8:00 p.m. in the evening. He was not killing himself on just a few hours of sleep; he was getting a good eight hours of sleep every night. Actually, he was insistent on getting that much sleep. I was serving college students on a college schedule and trying to get up at 4:00 a.m., and it was killing me. It sure would have been nice if those more seasoned ministers had filled me in on that little

Section II—The Power

fact. (Side note: I later found out these other young ministers had only been trying to keep Wesley's schedule for a short time and were also unable to keep it up. I learned that if you are going to listen to someone, make sure whatever it is they are suggesting has been working for them for more than a few weeks.)

I then began to think about all the other standards or "ought to's" that I was hearing at conferences and reading in books. Read the Bible, meditate, pray, make time to talk with and cultivate your relationship with your wife, practice the discipline of fasting, witness, fellowship, manage your finances superbly, take care of your material things as a good steward, exercise, be involved in your local community, build your faith, grow in love, take every thought captive, resist the devil, put on the full armor of God—and do it all *daily*. I realized if I did everything everyone said to do daily, I would have a checklist a mile long. It just did not seem like Jesus followed a huge checklist everyday, yet right before He died, He said He had accomplished all the Father had given Him to do (John 17:4).

What does all this have to do with life change and what we discussed in the last chapter? I am convinced, according to Jesus example and life experience, that the best way to change and grow is by the power and the leading of the Holy Spirit. In the last chapter, we discussed how Paul said that the way out of the sin "rut" was by putting on Christ (His "suit") and living in the power of His Holy Spirit. In that same solution oriented chapter, Paul then takes a good amount of time to elaborate on what it means to live in the Spirit's power with the goal of being "led" by the Spirit (Romans 8:14).

Jesus said He only did what He saw the Father doing (John 5:19). Jesus could have been doing a thousand good

Chapter 3 • The Mind and the Holy Spirit

things with His limited time in Israel, yet, instead of trying to do it all, He followed the leading of God's Spirit so He only did what God wanted Him to do. When all is said and done, doing what God wants done is the only thing that will matter. 1 John 2:17 tells us everything of the flesh will pass away, but the person who does God's will lasts forever. Jesus would sometimes say no to what people wanted Him to do and other times He said yes. Sometimes He would heal one person, sometimes the whole crowd. On a few occasions, He multiplied food, but He did not do it every day. Jesus lived in the constant flow of God's river of life, because He was perfectly led by the Spirit in God's plan and will for each day. That is the ideal for us as well. We will not be as on-target as Jesus, who was God in the flesh and sinless with perfect spiritual perception and sight, but we can get better and better at it, as we practice what the Bible teaches.

Notice what Paul says, as we continue in Romans 8, about living in the Spirit's power. "Those who live according to the sinful nature have their minds set on what that nature desires; but those who live in accordance with the Spirit have their minds set on what the Spirit desires" (Romans 8:5 NIV). In the middle of his discourse on living in the Spirit's power, Paul addresses the mind; specifically our mindset. This is the third "S" in God's solution to busting out of your rut.

3. Change Your Mind(s)et

God tells us that, in order to live in the life of the Holy Spirit, we need to change our mental focus from what the sinful nature desires to what the Holy Spirit desires. We are all familiar with the phrase, "quiet on the set." In the movie and theater arena, the "set" is the place where the scene is

Section II—The Power

played out. It is the place of focus for all who are working on the project and eventually for all who will be entertained by it. When the set is changed, it means a change in the story is taking place. It is the same with the set of our minds.

What we set our minds on, focus on, or dwell on becomes a deciding factor in rut busting or rut living. Ephesians 4:17–18 (NIV) says, "So I tell you this, and insist on it in the Lord, that you must no longer live as the Gentiles do, in the futility of their thinking. They are darkened in their understanding and separated from the life of God because of the ignorance that is in them due to the hardening of their heart." Paul uses very forceful language here, saying, "I insist on it in the Lord." In other words he is saying, "You have to get this, you have to understand it and practice this. Even though you now have a new, God-recreated nature, you can still miss out on the life of God, like the lost do, if you practice wrong thinking." The lost have hardened their hearts to God, which produces dark thinking, which leads to separation from the life of God. When we receive Jesus, our heart is made soft, but our minds still need to be renewed for transformation and Godly life to be our experience. Romans 12:2 tells us this world has a pattern, a way of thinking and acting, that tries to force us into its mold. We are not to conform to that pattern anymore, but rather, we are to renew our minds through God's word, and that, in turn, will transform us and change us to be more like Jesus.

The mind is one of the main gates through which the Holy Spirit will flow to bring life change. If we choose to think on things the old nature wants, we will shut down the flow of the Spirit in our lives; in a sense, bottling up His influence. Continued wrong thinking will eventually build

Chapter 3 • The Mind and the Holy Spirit

up mind and soul strongholds, patterns, and habits of thinking and responding that will dominate the "set" of our minds. However, if we open our minds and train them to think on God, His words, His truth, and to look at life according to His ideas, the Holy Spirit's power will flow into us and through us to liberate and release us.

We have all experienced this to one degree or another. If we start thinking about how awful the world is, how terrible people have been to us, or how unfair life is, if we focus on all our mistakes, shameful experiences, and the opportunities we've blown, it will not take long before we are sitting in a dark, gloomy hole. It may be sunny all around, but we will not see it because of the darkness we have been staring at. However, if we change the set of our minds and begin to focus on the beautiful nature of God, the numerous ways we have already been blessed, the awesome promises He has given us, the significant ways He is using us, the great ways people have treated us, and the power of the Holy Spirit in us, light begins to fill our souls.

I picture it like a dam. Normally, a constructed dam blocks a river so that the water is higher on one side than on the other. At certain times, the water is released to flow through the dam. The water provides enough force to power large devices, which then provide electrical power for us to use. The water is like the power of the Holy Spirit, and the generators are like our minds. As we focus our minds on the words of God and the things pleasing to Him, the Holy Spirit flows through our minds and produces power to change. Often feelings follow focus, so if we change what our minds are set on, Holy Spirit inspired emotions and virtues will be our experience.

Another way the word *set* is used is as a medical term, like to set a bone. On my thirteenth birthday, I broke a bone

Section II—The Power

in my forearm; an unforgettable present. I went to the doctor and he had to set it. I will never forget the feeling as he pushed the cracked bones into place before he put the cast on. It really hurt, but it was necessary if I did not want to go through life with a crooked arm.

The sin and negative experiences of life can bend, break, and warp our souls and our thinking. Many of us will continue in life, missing out on the life of God, if we do not get our thinking set in the right way. It does take some effort and practice, and it is sometimes uncomfortable or even painful to take broken thinking and set it right. God will not do this for us, but He will help us with it. He will help us recognize wrong beliefs and thinking and then help us reset our thinking to be in line with His revealed truth, which then releases soul-changing power in us.

The key to doing this is found in Romans 8:6–7 (NIV). "The mind of sinful man is death, but the mind controlled by the Spirit is life and peace; the sinful mind is hostile to God. It does not submit to God's law, nor can it do so."

Continuing, the next "S" is:

4. Submit to God's Words

I know that no one likes the word "submit," especially in the land of the free. We do not like anyone telling us what to do. Saying you submit is like admitting defeat to a dominating, stronger foe. We do not like to lose or yield to anyone, but, as Bob Dylan correctly sang years ago, "you're gonna serve somebody." We are either submitting to sin and thus the devil, or we are submitting to God. Some say, "I'm my own man. I do not submit or yield to anyone." I have news for you, with that attitude you are automatically serving sin and the devil. You see the sin-dominated mind is contrary to God, His standards, and His

Chapter 3 • The Mind and the Holy Spirit

word. Sin is a God rebel, wanting to go its own selfish, death-producing way. If we yield to it, as Paul wrote in Ephesians, we'll miss out on the life of God. If, however, we train our minds to submit to God and His words then life and peace will be our experience.

What does that mean and how do we do it? It simply means choosing to receive what God says and rejecting what sin says. For example, 1 Corinthians 10:13 (NIV) says, "No temptation has seized you except as is common to man. And God is faithful; he will not let you be tempted beyond what you can bear. But when you are tempted, he will also provide a way out so that you can stand up under it." When I am faced with a temptation I do not rebel against what God says by complaining, "This temptation is just too strong. I cannot beat it. It beats me. I just give up." That is submitting to the devil's words, not God's. Instead, I say, "This temptation is not anything unusual. People all around me have been facing this type of thing for years. God is always faithful. He will provide a way out for me and I'm going to see it and be able to do it." That is submitting to God's words and that will produce life and peace in us.

When hate, lust, or vengeful thoughts come knocking on the door of our minds, it is possible to open the door to them and welcome them in for a time of internal conversation and fellowship. If we do this, though, they will not be nice guests. Like some "friends" or relatives, they will try to move in with you, and then they will try to take over your home. Do not submit to them; leave them outside. Instead, Jesus said He knocks at the door, and if we let Him in, He will have fellowship with us (Revelation 3:20). If we listen to Him and let His presence fill our internal homes, then God's life will increasingly fill our souls.

Section II—The Power

If you practice setting your mind and submitting to what pleases God; that will help you do the fifth, and final, "S":

5. Be Sensitive to the Spirit

Romans 8:14–15 (NLT) says, "For all who are led by the Spirit of God are children of God. So you should not be like cowering, fearful slaves. You should behave instead like God's very own children, adopted into his family— calling him, 'Father, dear Father.'" There is absolutely no substitute for the Holy Spirit. The Holy Spirit is the presence of God on earth. He is the one who convinces people of their need for the Savior, Jesus (John 16:7–11). He causes spiritual rebirth and recreation to happen (Titus 3:5–6). He makes a relationship with God the Father and Jesus possible while we are still on earth (John 14:16–21, 1 John 1:3). He teaches believers God's truth and reveals God's riches (1 Corinthians 2:8–13, John 14:26). It is the Holy Spirit who empowers Christians to be witnesses of Jesus (Acts 1:8). He develops Christ-like character in people, called the fruits of the Spirit (Galatians 5:22–23). He does supernatural works of God through believers, called "Gifts of the Spirit" (1 Corinthians 12:7–11). The church got started, and is still going today, only by the presence and power of the Holy Spirit. Jesus Himself did not start His public ministry until the Holy Spirit came upon Him. Jesus said all He did was by the Holy Spirit's power.

God has a transformation plan for each one of us. He knows the insights we need, the miracles, the challenges, the victories, and even the defeats. He knows what needs to be worked on and in what order. If we simply try to improve ourselves, when God is not working in that area, we will see very little progress. If however, we learn to be sen-

Chapter 3 • The Mind and the Holy Spirit

sitive to the Holy Spirit and give effort where God is at work, we are then partnering with Him and the results will be real and significant.

Once I realized that, even though there are countless good things I could be working on, the only thing that really mattered was listening to Jesus and doing what He said, my life got a lot better. If you're familiar with the New Testament at all, you will remember the story of Mary and Martha. Luke tells the story in chapter 10:38–41. Jesus comes to Martha and Mary's home with a fairly large number of people. Martha is busy taking care of all the guests, but Mary is sitting with the men, listening to Jesus. Martha is upset by this and asks Jesus to get Mary to help her. Jesus says to her, "Martha, dear Martha, you're fussing far too much and getting yourself worked up over nothing. One thing is essential, and Mary has chosen it—it's the main course, and won't be taken from her" (Luke 10:41 The Message). Jesus is not telling us to be lazy and do nothing with our lives. He was definitely a man of action, and so were His closest followers, but the order is crucial. Martha was stressed out over doing what she thought was important. Jesus said Mary made a choice, as we need to as well, for the one main thing, the essential thing, is listening to Jesus first. Notice, Jesus said "it won't be taken from her." When we, by the indwelling Holy Spirit, choose to sit first and listen to Jesus, and then live and work on what He says, it will not be taken away from us, it will produce lasting results. That is true of ministry and it is true of life change.

It takes practice to learn what is the Holy Spirit's leading and what is not. You will make mistakes, but God is so gracious to people who are sincerely trying. That is what we are going to look at in the next chapter, but before we do, let's review and summarize.

Section II—The Power

To get out of that negative sin rut:

1. Put on God's Suit (Jesus).
2. Live in the Spirit's Power.
3. Change Your Mindset.
4. Submit to God.
5. Develop Sensitivity to the Holy Spirit.

Chapter 4
Following God's Lead

A few years ago, I was attending a church service in another town. During the worship time, a clear thought jumped in my mind just as my attention fell on a woman across the room: "Tell her I know where she is. I have not forgotten her." Now I am just like you, I get all types of thoughts going through my mind throughout the day. Some of them are noble, others are dumb, and others are just plain awful. I realize not every thought I get comes from God, but some do. Over the years I have had thoughts like this from time to time that did end up coming from God; helping people come to Christ or giving them real encouragement, strength, or answers. So I decided to give it a shot. If this thought was from God, it might really help her; if it is not from Him, at least I tried. So at the end of the service I went up to her and said, "I know you do not know me and this might sound strange to you, but this thought

Section II—The Power

came to my mind during worship for you. Would you listen and tell me what you think?" I guess I did not look too weird, plus, this was a church that taught God is still alive and can still communicate with us today, so she said, "Sure. Go ahead." I shared the thoughts that had come to my mind as naturally as I could, being careful not to add or take anything away. After I shared them, she got this happy, surprised look on her face and said very enthusiastically, "That is exactly right. I have just gone through a situation where I was wondering if God had forgotten about me; if He even knew where I was. Who are you?"

As you can imagine I felt totally pumped. I really did hear something from God that I had no way of knowing, and it really seemed to help her. I kept my composure and, trying to be humble, said something like, "I'm just a pastor from another town. One of God's kids trying to encourage another one." Then I coolly walked away to talk with some friends across the room. On the outside I was acting calm, but on the inside I was so excited because it was another example of the reality of a living, active, and loving God giving someone just what they needed at just the right time. This is terrible and it goes to show how much television sticks with us, but I kind of felt like I was the Lone Ranger after he had saved the day. As he rode off into the sunset there would always be one person asking another, "Who was that masked man?" They always said, "Why, that's the Lone Ranger." That is how I felt when that young lady said, "Who are you?" I was the mighty hero saving the day and trying to act cool about it. Maybe that is why God does not give me those types of words all the time.

This was, at least for me, a dramatic example of the Holy Spirit's ability to communicate what God is doing at a particular time. In the last chapter we talked about being

Chapter 4 • Following God's Lead

sensitive to the Holy Spirit's leading as the key to God-empowered transformation, as well as effective ministry. We discussed the fact that when we focus on what God is focusing on, then God grants grace and power to accomplish His will. When we try to do just any good idea that comes to mind, we cannot see long lasting change happen because our strength just does not hold up in these tough to change areas of life. So it is wonderful to know that God desires to guide us and show us where He is working so we can work with Him.

Right before He went to the cross, Jesus told his disciples, "And I will ask the Father, and he will give you another Counselor to be with you forever—the Spirit of truth" (John 14:16 NIV). He continued, "All this I have spoken while still with you. But the Counselor, the Holy Spirit, whom the Father will send in my name, will teach you all things and remind you of everything I have said to you" (John 14:25–26 NIV). The disciples had just spent three years with Jesus in person. They were naturally unsettled when He told them He would be leaving, so Jesus gave them these comforting and expectancy-producing words. God was going to give them a divine Counselor who was like Jesus, the Holy Spirit. He said that this Counselor would be with all believers forever and that He would teach us, remind us, and counsel us the same way Jesus did.

After His death and resurrection, we see this is exactly what happened in the life of the early church. In Acts 11:12 (NIV), the Apostle Peter was explaining to the other church leaders why he went to Caesarea and preached the gospel message to this particular group of people. Peter said, "The Spirit told me to have no hesitation about going with them." Acts 13 tells us the first missionaries to the non-Jewish world were sent out by the direct guidance of the

Section II—The Power

Holy Spirit: "While they were worshiping the Lord and fasting, the Holy Spirit said, 'Set apart for me Barnabas and Saul for the work to which I have called them.'" In both of these instances, the Holy Spirit clearly communicated to these Christ followers and showed them where God was working, and what God wanted them to do. He will do the same today, if we learn how to recognize His leading.

So how do we recognize the Holy Spirit's voice? As I said, every day we get all kinds of thoughts journeying through our minds. Which ones are from God? Which ones are from the devil? Which ones are inspired by what we want, or by the movie we just watched, the book we read, or that spicy Burrito we had for lunch? How do we know? That is what we're going to look at right now.

It starts with parameters. Scripture teaches us to be open and receptive, but not gullible. 1 Thessalonians 5:19–22 (NIV) says, "Do not put out the Spirit's fire; do not treat prophecies with contempt. Test everything. Hold on to the good. Avoid every kind of evil." Comedian Lily Tomlin once said, "Why is it when we talk to God we're praying, but when God talks to us, we're schizophrenic?" She makes a good point, but we also understand why people are skeptical. People who "hear voices" or "hear God" often do bizarre, and sometimes awful, things. This Scripture gives us the right balance. Stay open to God, but do not believe every thought or idea is from Him. We are to test the words we hear.

There are two main tests we can use:

1. **Is this glorifying Jesus Christ?** 1 John 4:1–3a (NIV) says, "Dear friends, do not believe every spirit, but test the spirits to see whether they are from God, because many false prophets have gone

Chapter 4 • Following God's Lead

out into the world. This is how you recognize the Spirit of God: Every spirit that acknowledges that Jesus Christ has come in the flesh is from God, but every spirit that does not acknowledge Jesus is not from God." That is pretty clear, isn't it? Every spirit, thought, idea, message, experience that does not acknowledge Jesus is not from God. If it glorifies or draws people to any other leader, teacher, angel, philosophy, or religion it is not the Holy Spirit. The Holy Spirit will always draw people to Jesus Christ and glorify Him.

In Acts 14, Paul was preaching in Lystra when, through His words, God healed a crippled man. The pagan people of that city began calling Paul and Barnabas *gods* because of this miracle. That still happens today sometimes when miracles are performed. In their own minds, pagan people often try to make the messenger divine. However, Paul would have none of that. He pointed directly and immediately to Jesus as the Savior and doer of miracles, not himself. Every true teacher, every God-inspired thought, every divine experience, will always point back to, and ultimately give glory to, Jesus Christ.

2. **Is it in line with the teachings of the Bible?** In John 17:17 (NIV) Jesus prayed for all His followers, "Sanctify them by the truth; your word is truth." The Holy Spirit will never tell us to do anything contrary to God's word. God knew there would be all types of words and thoughts going through our minds, so He gave us something specific that we could use as a filter to sift through it all and come out with the gold of His words and ideas.

Section II—The Power

When I was in college, I read an article in the Memphis paper about a woman who said she was a stripper for Jesus. The article reported how she was convinced God had given her this gift and she was using it to glorify God and to bless people. I think it is safe to say, she was not listening to the Holy Spirit. Scripture tells us not to do anything that would cause our brother to stumble and this act on her part certainly could have this outcome. Test the thoughts with the Bible. By the way, that means you need to get to know it pretty well. Keep reading it, studying it, and meditating on it, and you will be able to discern more and more when God is talking to you and when a message is coming from somewhere else.

Next, it helps to understand the possibilities. As we have already seen, the Bible teaches that the Holy Spirit is inside each and every believer. That means the greatest percentage of guidance by the Holy Spirit will be inside us and come to us through our minds and emotions. Even when God does give external guidance, there still needs to be an inner conviction that this is what God wants us to know or do. This is a learning process because these inner impulses can be very subjective. Maybe you can relate to the little girl who was sent to her room by her mother. After a few minutes, the mother went in to talk with her about what she had done. Teary eyed, the little darling said, "Why do we do wrong, Mommy?" The mother responded, "Sometimes the devil tells us to do something wrong and we listen to him. We need to listen to God instead." The little girl sobbed, "But God doesn't talk loud enough." Sometimes we feel that way, don't we? Stick with it, though, we can all learn to hear God's voice.

Chapter 4 • Following God's Lead

Here are some of the major ways, or possibilities, that God uses to speak to us:

1. **Clear thoughts.** 2 Timothy 2:7 (NIV) says, "Reflect on what I am saying, for the Lord will give you insight into all this." In my experience, the most common way God speaks to us is through our natural thinking processes. For a while, I thought I always had to have a major, out of the blue "word," like I had for that young woman, in order to be doing God's will. However, the majority of the time, when I pray and ask God, "What do you want me to do?" I get silence or several random thoughts. Sometimes I do get a clear, no doubt about it, God-has-spoken word, but that is not nearly as common as getting clarity due to reflection. After a while, I realized that if I sat around and waited for one of those types of revelations before I did anything, I would spend most of my life just sitting around. It helped me so much when, reading Acts, I saw how Paul did not always have a specific word about every single action he took in life. He had habits and patterns he regularly followed. Often he would go out in the public arena and talk with anyone who happened to be there (not getting a clear, specific word on who to talk to and who not to talk to), and God worked powerfully through him. He obeyed what God had already made clear to him and then followed His God-focused, ministry-minded thoughts.

    Sometimes, really fairly often, God does give us those crystal-clear, the lights go on, dramatic words. I love those times, but they do not come nearly as often as sanctified thinking.

Section II—The Power

2. **Mental pictures.** A couple of years ago, I saw an interview on a Christian television show with a surgeon who just could not figure out what was wrong with his patient. Despite performing every test he and his team could think of, he just could not find the problem. One day, while praying, he had a mental picture of what the problem was. The patient gave the okay for exploratory surgery, and when the doctor did the surgery, he saw the problem just as he had seen in his mind while praying. It solved the problem. God can communicate with you this way as well.

3. **Dreams.** Scripture gives numerous accounts, in both the Old and New Testament, of God communicating with people through dreams. In some cases, He continues to reveal things in this way today. For example, in the fall of 2004, the *Seattle Times* reported an amazing story regarding God speaking this way. On October 2, 2004, seventeen-year-old Laura Hatch left a party in a Seattle neighborhood, and that was the last time she was seen for over a week. More than two hundred volunteers searched tirelessly for her, but to no avail. One night, however, a member of Laura's church, named Sha Nohr, had trouble sleeping. She kept having a recurring dream of a wooded area and heard the message, "Keep going, keep going." The following morning she and her daughter drove to the area she saw in her dream, praying along the way. She said that something drew her to stop and clamber over a concrete barrier. More than one hundred feet down a steep, densely vegetated embankment she barely managed to discern the crumpled 1996 Toyota

Chapter 4 • Following God's Lead

Camry that Laura drove. Nohr discovered Laura in the back seat, conscious, but seriously injured. Laura was taken to the hospital where she was treated for serious injuries and dehydration, but she lived. God can speak to you in dreams. Once again, are all dreams from God? No, but they can be.

4. **Emotional connections**. Many times you cannot explain it, but you just "know" you should do something. One time Janet and I were talking with a man we had recently met. He told us he was going to meet a friend. As he walked away, we both turned to each other and said, "His friend is gay and he is being tempted with it." We later talked with our friend about it and he admitted he was struggling in that direction, but did not want to give in to it. We prayed with him, God did a work, and he has been happily married for almost twenty years now. How did we know? We just knew, by the Spirit of God. Other emotional connections you'll find in Scripture are things like great love or compassion (Mark 1:41), faith or boldness greater than your own (Acts 4:31), a strong desire that sticks with you (Psalm 37:4), or a great peace despite contrary circumstances (Romans 8:6).

Internal guidance should be the main indicator of what God wants us to know and do, but He does regularly use external indicators as well. For example, God often uses circumstances to get our attention. If I am regularly getting into fights and disputes wherever I go, there is a good chance that God wants me to get to the root of that problem. If your spouse is telling you about some areas of your life that are negative or hurtful, there is a good chance that

Section II—The Power

God is speaking to you through her. At church, you will often hear teachings that are talking to you, and you know it. If you keep getting speeding tickets, there is a good chance that God is trying to talk to you about your lifestyle. On occasion, another Christian will share something with you as I did with that woman. These and many other externals can be used by God to talk to us, but they should ring an internal bell; you may have to think about it, or pray about it, but if it is from God, then there will be an inner "yes."

One last point that is very important, and it relates to our chapter on "Changing Your Theme Song," is putting God first in your life. I have taken several pages to make the point about internal connections and hearing a "yes" in your soul. To do that, it is crucial that you are putting God first with a "not my will, but Yours be done" attitude. In John 7:17, Jesus said if we are willing to do God's will, we will know if teaching, thoughts, or ideas are from God. When the prophet Jonah was told by God to go to Ninevah and give them His message, he did not have an internal yes, because he hated the people of that area, in fact they were enemies, so he took a boat and went in another direction! When Jonah was thrown overboard and swallowed by a whale, God definitely got his attention. Spending time in the belly of a whale had a way of helping him to change his tune, and got him willing to do what God wanted done. Once Jonah said, "Your will be done, Lord," God had the whale spit him out close to Ninevah, and Jonah did what God wanted done. The point is, in order to hear clearly, we need to make sure we are keeping God first in our lives and are willing to do whatever He says, whenever He says to do it. Psalm 37:4 says that God does give us the desires of our hearts, but the condition is to delight ourselves in Him.

Chapter 4 • Following God's Lead

When we keep Him first, we will hear correctly much more often and make far fewer mistakes. We will still make them, as we are not perfect, but we do this far less than if we get our priorities out of order.

You can hear God! The Holy Spirit does speak to you! Follow Him and His grace will be there to bring lasting life change and powerful results.

Section III—The Process

Chapter I
How God Works

In 2001, something remarkable happened at the Super Bowl. It was not just that the New England Patriots pulled off one of the greatest upsets in Super Bowl history, but it is how they did it. They did something that coaches have been talking to their teams about ever since team sports began, but the Patriots actually pulled it off. It is called "teamwork." In our narcissistic age, the Patriots internalized and demonstrated the idea that "team comes before me (the individual)."

Intentionally, symbolically, they set this idea in motion even before the game began. Up to this time, at pregame introductions, each player from the starting offense and defense would run out, one at a time, as their name was called over the public address system. The crowd would cheer wildly for each individual player as they soaked in the glory of their achievement; playing in a Super Bowl before

Section III—The Process

a worldwide audience. The New England Patriots had none of that. In an unprecedented move, when it came time to introduce their players, the entire team ran onto the field at once. I remember watching on television and thinking, "something powerful is going on here." It sent such a clear message to the St. Louis Rams, their opponent, and to everyone watching: "we are first and foremost a team, not a group of individual stars." Despite being huge underdogs, they won the game and have continued to model this philosophy year after year.

Studies show that a team that truly functions as a team usually outperforms an individual. In order for teamwork to happen, the members have to know how to work with each other—not just next to each other, or, still worse, against one another. This is true of any organization and it is true in partnering with God. He already knows us better than we know ourselves. He knows how we function, when we need encouragement, when we need comfort, and when we need a kick in the seat of the pants. We are the ones who need to learn how God works if we are going to be His teammates and coworkers.

There is no way, with our limited minds, that we can understand everything about God, or why or how He does what He does. However, we can know enough to cooperate with Him as He works in our lives and in the world around us. In this chapter, we are going to look at one of the main ways God works. As we understand this, we can cooperate with Him and play as a real team with Him. What an honor God has afforded us by allowing us to play on His championship team and actually make important contributions to what He is doing. Let's start with 2 Peter 1:3–4 (NASB), which says, "seeing that His divine power has granted to us everything pertaining to life and godliness, through the true

Chapter I • How God Works

knowledge of Him who called us by His own glory and excellence. For by these He has granted to us His precious and magnificent promises, so that by them you may become partakers of the divine nature, having escaped the corruption that is in the world by lust."

These God-inspired words tell us we can actually partake, participate in, and share in God's nature. We are certainly not divine, but it is very possible to participate in God's overwhelming love, His joy and peace, His faith and courage, and His righteousness and holiness. I have read these words for years, yet it is still incredible to me that God wants me to experience the nature He, Himself, has, and He has already made it available to me! It is not just for a few special people, either, it is God's will for all of us. When I realize how wonderful God is, the force of life that is in Him, the quality of existence He enjoys, and that He wants me to share in it, it really does make me want to fall on my knees in thanks and worship and then get out there and let others know what kind of life is possible.

If that is not yet your experience, these verses should be very helpful to you. They show us the way we experience this life is 1) through knowing Jesus (verse 3), and 2) seeing and receiving the promises God gives (verse 4). God's promises are described as "precious and magnificent," very great, rich, precious, and of great worth and value. It is by these promises that we share in the divine nature. If we want to participate in God's life-changing power, it will normally include personally receiving His promises.

God's words and His promises are precious and magnificent, and a means for us to experience His nature because they flow in perfect harmony from who He is. God is awesome and His life-producing words are expressions of that nature. The Bible is filled with thousands of power-

Section III—The Process

packed, need-meeting promises. No one forced God to give us these promises. There was no negotiation where the human race said, "God, if you will promise to do all these things, then we will do our part." No! God Almighty, of His own volition, out of His own nature, spoke words of promise saying, "This is my will for you. This is what I want you to have." 2 Corinthians 1:19–20 (NIV) says, "For the Son of God, Jesus Christ, who was preached among you by me and Silas and Timothy, was not 'Yes' and 'No', but in him it has always been 'Yes'. For no matter how many promises God has made, they are 'Yes' in Christ." God does not waver back and forth in what He has said and promised. He says yes to His promises for everyone who has received Jesus because those words are an expression of who He is, and His actions always line up with His words.

Unfortunately, our nature and our words do not always line up. Sometimes we say the wrong things. How many of us have said something and the very second it went out of our mouth, we knew it was not good? We wished to God that we could reel those words right back in our mouth before they landed with a thud or cause an explosion. Our actions do not always line up with our words; we do not always perfectly practice what we preach. I remember when my boys were young, I spoke at church on Philippians 4:6–7, which tells us not to worry, and instead pray with thanksgiving and God's peace will actually guard our hearts and minds in Christ Jesus. On the way home from the service I was telling Janet how concerned I was about a situation, when from the back seat a little voice said, "Dad, what about Philippians 4:6–7? Why don't you pray instead of getting worried?" I was busted by a little kid from my own home who was not yet big enough to see over the steering

Chapter 1 • How God Works

wheel. At least he was listening. The point is, I am not always consistent in what I say and do; but God is.

A majority of the time, God works through His words. Often in Scripture, we see God first declaring something, then at some later point it comes to pass. Isaiah 55:10–11 (NLT) explains it so well, "The rain and the snow come down from the heavens and stay on the ground to water the earth. They cause the grain to grow, producing seed for the farmer and bread for the hungry. It is the same with my word. I send it out, and it always produces fruit. It will accomplish all I want it to and it will prosper everywhere I send it." Notice the verb "send." God sees His spoken words as being sent from Him to a situation. These words carry God's life and power to produce all He wants them to accomplish. His words are so power-packed that they always produce fruit and they prosper no matter where He sends them. I have never seen rain or snow make contact with the ground without making it wetter than before the rain or snow came. It happens every single time. It is the same with the words, the promises God has spoken, they will do what He sends them to do every single time, if received. I will address this further in the next chapter.

Genesis 1:1–2 (NIV) tells us, "In the beginning God created the heavens and the earth. Now the earth was formless and empty, darkness was over the surface of the deep, and the Spirit of God was hovering over the waters." How did God change the earth into something alive and beautiful from a dark, empty mass? He spoke words! He said, "Let there be light" and those words produced light in the darkness. Each day, for six days, God said, "let there be" and there was. It was not there before He spoke, but once He did, it came into existence. Can you imagine the power it took to create the force of light in the universe? Light is

Section III—The Process

able to travel at 186,000 miles per second from one end of the universe to the other. The power to bring the force of life into an empty, lifeless mass, with such order and energy that it keeps producing thousands of years later; that is the power in God's words and that is the power in His promises.

Paul writes about it again in 2 Corinthians 4:6 (NASB) regarding us, "For God, who said, 'Light shall shine out of darkness' is the One who has shone in our hearts to give the Light of the Knowledge of the glory of God in the face of Christ." Paul uses the same wording, the Creation analogy, to describe how God puts spiritual, eternal life in us. We, like the formless, dark earth, were spiritually dead, dark, and empty. Then God spoke words into us, the Light of the Knowledge of the glory of God came into our spirits as we looked to Jesus. We were recreated, spiritually, by the same powerful words that created light.

This pattern is repeated throughout Scripture. God spoke words of promise then, at some point, they happened in our world. Sometimes it took just seconds, or perhaps a nanosecond, as when Jesus raised Lazarus from the dead. Jesus stood at the open grave, did not even go in, but simply sent words of power saying, "Lazarus, come forth." Those Spirit-empowered words carried enough life in them to raise Lazarus from the dead. Other times, it took generations before the promise was fulfilled, before the words He sent accomplished what He sent them to do. God told Abraham that his descendants would live in the Promised Land, but it took over four hundred years before that happened. At Pentecost, Peter told the crowd that what they were seeing and hearing (as the first one hundred and twenty church members were baptized in the Holy Spirit and were praising God in tongues, or languages they had

Chapter 1 • How God Works

never learned) was the fulfillment of the promise that God had given through the prophet Joel hundreds of years before. What they were seeing was the fulfillment of those words of life and power that God had spoken long before.

This is how God works. His word carries His power to do what He wants done. In Luke 8, Jesus described God's words as God's seed. A seed always carries the nature of the life form that produced it. We all know an apple tree will only produce apple seeds, which in turn will grow into an apple tree. We know it will never produce a banana or orange tree; it will produce after its nature. God's word will only produce in us His nature, never anything else.

It should become obvious to us that if we want to grow and change, then the seed of God's word needs to be planted in our hearts. If it is planted in good soil, it will produce God fruit. On the other hand, if there is no God-seed there can be no life of God. 1 Peter 1:23 (NASB) says, "for you have been born again, not of seed which is perishable but imperishable, that is, through the living and abiding word of God." Every person who has received Jesus through the Gospel has a new God-created nature. We have an imperishable, indestructible God-seed in us that is "living and abiding." That means it will keep on working and keep on producing divine fruit; divine nature in us.

The seed illustration is so helpful because seeds, generally, grow slowly. There is always a period of time after the seed is planted during which it appears that nothing is really happening. Appearances can be deceiving, however, because in the unseen realm under the earth's surface change is occurring. That seed is growing and expanding and, at some point, its growth will be seen when it penetrates the top layer of earth. In some instances, it can take a long time before any growth is visible. One of the most

Section III—The Process

spectacular examples in nature is the Chinese bamboo tree. Once the seed is planted, even with optimal care, nothing visible is seen for approximately seven years. Then, within hours and days, it begins an incredible, visible growth process. From seemingly nothing, these trees can grow over one hundred feet in a matter of days; but for seven years it looks like nothing is changing.

Most trees have a steadier, more gradual growth track; but even then, growth is barely noticeable when measured by hours or days. It is seen much more clearly over months and years. The same can often be said of us. We do have some areas of our lives that show rapid growth and change, but, more often, growth and change is more gradual and steady. God's seed is growing though, and will produce something powerful and strong, precious and magnificent, in our lives. Scripture does not call us weeds of God; instead, it calls us "oaks of righteousness, the planting of the Lord."

If we want to cooperate with God, play on His team, and work with Him, it will always involve His words, His seeds. There can be little or no lasting God-empowered transformation without His words. However, with them, the divine nature can progressively be our experience.

How do we receive from God? How do we work with His words? That is in the next chapter.

Chapter 2
Receiving from God

    Janet and I moved to Germany as missionaries in our early twenties. Those years give us many memories because we were just starting out in ministry and we had so many unique experiences. Even though Germany is western culture, there are still major differences in beliefs, customs, and worldview, not to mention language. One of the more enjoyable differences is the role that bread plays in that country.

    You cannot be in Germany for long without realizing the Germans are bread experts. There are quaint little bakeries everywhere and these bakeries do not just have pastries and cakes, but also bread. They have more types of bread than you would ever think possible; different sizes, colors, shapes, textures, densities, and tastes. When Jesus, the master communicator, said, "I am the bread of life," every German could relate well to His words.

Section III—The Process

Even with an abundance of awesome bakeries, some people still enjoy baking their own bread. At first, the church we started in Munich reached mainly young people. Some were from pretty wild backgrounds, living "alternative" lifestyles; pot smoking, don't buy into the system, casual to eastern styles of clothing, and sometimes communal living arrangements would describe many of them. Several people from this background who came to Christ invited Janet and me over for a little fellowship one day. The two young ladies and young man who invited us served tea and some homemade bread. They proudly handed a loaf to us, telling us it was whole corn bread that they had made themselves out of only natural ingredients. When they handed it to me, I could not believe that bread could be so heavy. It felt like a brick in my hand. I knew if I threw it and hit someone, that brick of bread could cause some major damage. They got out this turbo charged, heavy duty, super electric bread cutter and cut off some pieces and, along with some butter, passed them to us. With a whole lot of chewing, we did eat it and actually enjoyed it, but it was so substantive that eating just a piece or two filled us up. I had no idea that bread could be so heavy and filling. No wonder Germans think American bread is almost an abomination to "breadhood," so wimpy and limp.

There are hundreds of types of bread, but they all must have some of the same common ingredients to be classified as bread. In the same way, God has many different ways to help us, but they generally involve some of the same main ingredients. God's ingredients are much more substantive and lasting than any ingredients our world can offer. We have looked at several already, but in this chapter I want to focus on one key ingredient that is almost always involved in receiving God's power to change. If you have been a

Chapter 2 • Receiving from God

Christian for anytime at all, it is one you have heard of quite a bit, but I ask you to keep on reading because I am trusting that you may gain some fresh insights or at least confirmation on how you look at it; it's called faith.

Often, when faith is discussed, people have one or two of these reactions:

1. I do not have enough faith. (I feel condemned and/or hopeless.)
2. Yes, faith is the key to absolutely everything related to God. (It is all you need. If something is not working, it is because you do not have enough faith.)
3. Faith is a set of rules that wore me out. (It was all about my faith, doing and believing just right all the time. One wrong word or prayer and God would not act. Please give me grace instead.)
4. Faith in God is a Jesus-focused virtue that makes it possible to connect with and receive God and His grace. (Good news.)

I want you to know up front that I do believe faith is essential in the Christian life, along with love and hope, with love being the greatest. It is a key ingredient in receiving God's life-changing power, but it is not a heavy, "I must believe and do everything just right" law that makes life harder rather than easier. I do not claim to have all insight into this important topic, but let's look at a few things I have learned and see if it helps you too.

"Tell me this one thing: How did you receive the Holy Spirit? Did you receive the Spirit by following the law? No, you received the Spirit because you heard the good News and believed it. You began your life in Christ by the Spirit. Now are you trying to make it complete by your own

Section III—The Process

power? That is foolish. Were all your experiences wasted? I hope not! Does God give you the Spirit and work miracles among you because you follow the law? No, he does these things because you heard the Good News and believed it." (Galatians 3:2–5 NCV) The Galatian believers faced some of the same challenges we do. They wanted to grow and change and wanted to live the way God wanted them to, which always has its challenges. Confusing the matter, they had teachers of the Jewish law telling them faith in Christ alone was not enough, they also needed to come back under the Old Testament law to go on to maturity and to be right with God.

Paul almost screams, "NO, NO, NO, NO! You were never, and never will be, right with God by your own efforts, but only and simply by believing the good news, the word of God about Jesus. If you go back under the Law, you come under the heavy burden of trying to make yourself right with God by your limited, always falling short efforts. That's a terrible way to live. You are made right with God by trusting in Jesus Christ. It's the same with going on to maturity, receiving the Holy Spirit and God's miracles; it is not by human endeavor, but by believing God's message."

Faith is how we connect with God and how we receive God's life changing words of grace and power, "For by grace you have been saved *through faith*; and that not of yourselves, it is the gift of God; not as a result of works, so that no one may boast." (Ephesians 2:8–9) "For I am not ashamed of the gospel; for it is the power of God for salvation to *everyone who believes . . .*" (Romans 1:16). At one point in our lives, all of us were separated from God. He was always around us and most of us had some type of God experience at some point in our lives, but we were never

Chapter 2 • Receiving from God

connected until a specific thing happened. Did we have to do all the right things or keep all the commandments? No. Did we need to pray a certain amount of time? No. Did we need to give more? No. One thing had to happen; we needed to believe the message about Jesus.

That one step did what nothing else could do. It connected us to God so His power and grace flowed into our lives giving us a new nature, assurance of eternal life, and opening up all His promises to us. I'll say it again; it was not working, not crying, not sacrificing, and not giving, it was simply believing that did it. We did not try to work up some great feeling; we did not try to talk ourselves into it. The Holy Spirit drew us, and we said yes to His words, and God did the work. Faith is the connection through which God's power is made available to us. This is true, not only in connecting with God in salvation but also in Christian growth. Paul said we receive God's Spirit and God's miracles, which includes His ability to change, through faith. Jesus said over and over again, "Be it done to you according to your faith" and wonderful transformations would happen. This is such wonderful news! The simple act of believing what God says, releases His power to flow in our lives and circumstances like nothing else can.

That is why John wrote, "Jesus' disciples saw him do many other miraculous signs besides the ones recorded in this book. But these are written so that you may believe that Jesus is the Messiah, the Son of God, and that by believing in him you will have life." (John 20:30–31 NLT) Ever since, the goal of the apostles and ministers is to give God's word with the assurance that every single person who receives it, by believing, will receive God's life. Just as it is crucial to understand God's word is His seed and with it God's life is present (see last chapter), it is also crucial to

Section III—The Process

realize the way those words are received is simply by believing them.

When we believe God's words, the Holy Spirit works, power is released, and miracles can happen. At least up to this point in my life, God has not graced me with great healing or miracle gifts, but every now and then I've seen these things happen first hand. On our first trip to Yugoslavia in the early 80s, the local pastor who invited us took us to the home of a man with an inoperable brain tumor. I'll never forget the poverty, which was never uncommon in a communist country. The tiny home they lived in was two very small rooms and the roof was so short I could not stand upright in most of the house (I'm not quite 6 feet tall). This man was not yet a Christ follower, but he was very desperate. We shared the good news with him that Jesus came to take the barrier away between him and a loving God and told him God did have the power to do miracles today. We prayed a simple prayer, he agreed with our prayer and then we left for another visit. The next day he went to Zagreb for more tests. A couple of days later the local pastor came to us excitedly telling us the tests showed the tumor was completely gone! We just prayed in simple faith and God did the work. Does it always happen that quickly and easily? I wish it did, but in my experience, those super quick manifestations are more the exception than the rule. I know God often performs instantaneous miracles, but most changes happen over time. Sometimes physical healing does not happen at all in this lifetime, but for sure, it does in the next. However, I am convinced, there are many, many times God wants to do great works in this life if we will simply believe Him.

Let's look at how this applies to life change and spiritual growth. Earlier we looked at 2 Peter 1:3–4 (NIV),

Chapter 2 • Receiving from God

which tells us God's divine power has given us everything we need for life and godliness through knowing Jesus. We also saw that the way we share in God's divine nature is through His promises and the way to receive God's promises, His words, is by simple faith. Verse 5 continues, "For this very reason, make every effort to add to your faith, goodness" then knowledge, self-control, perseverance, godliness, brotherly kindness, and love. Faith is the foundation because faith alone in Christ connects us with God. From this faith foundation, the platform from which we build, we then add these other important virtues. This is where it gets exciting and liberating because faith is not only the foundation, but it also plays a major role by which these important traits become part of us.

Peter writes believers should "add to your faith" Christ-like virtues. That means these virtues are not automatically there; they are lacking, not yet developed. How do we add what is lacking in our Christian character? We do need to "make every effort" as the text says, but if we do it in our own strength, it will become a "work of the flesh" that will end up wearing us out and leaving us feeling condemned. It is not enough to simply decide to be good or to have knowledge or self-control. Trying to add these virtues simply by trying harder or making a decision rarely holds up over time. So what do we do? How do we partner with God?

We give it our best ("make every effort") with specific faith in God to do it. I use the phrase "specific faith" because there are different types of faith, just like there are different expressions of love. General faith would be, "I believe God exists, I believe His word is true, I believe church is God's plan for every Christian, etc." Specific faith is, "I believe Jesus died for *my* sins. I believe God has

Section III—The Process

heard *this* prayer and will answer. I believe God is going to meet *this* need as I trust Him and obey Him." Much good happens through general faith, but some things require specific faith.

In John 12:36 (NASB) Jesus said, "While you have the Light, believe in the Light, so that you may become sons of Light." Did you notice those two key words: believe and become? Jesus said if we believe in Him as the Light, we become sons of Light. In other words, *believing leads to becoming.* Romans 4:18 says the same thing about Abraham, "In hope against hope he *believed*, so that he might *become* a father of many nations according to that which had been spoken." There it is again, believing leads to becoming. Abraham believed what God said about him and his future, and the text says his believing led to it becoming reality. Abraham did not just come up with a good idea and decided to believe God for it. Instead, he believed "according to that which had been spoken" by God (God's word, God's promise).

Abraham already had general faith, with some seasons of specific faith, on his journey with God. However, for this specific promise to come to pass, he needed to specifically believe it. When he believed God, even though it seemed impossible, God's power caused a miracle to occur. He eventually became the person God said He would. It is the same for us today. When we specifically take God's promises to us and receive them by faith, His power flows to make it happen because God stands behind His words. If we understand New Testament faith correctly, it is not a heavy load, it is liberating and heart lifting. When I trust God to do what He says, He releases power and resources to do what He said He would do. When I start exercising

Chapter 2 • Receiving from God

specific faith, based on His Holy Spirit inspired words, God does His work.

The question needs to be asked: Do I need to exercise specific faith in every area of my life all the time? No. Otherwise it would become one of those checklist things, putting all the pressure back on the individual. There are just too many areas of life to do this in. Part of God's "light yoke" is knowing that He is working and in charge of things we are not even aware of. He has the God job. We have the responsibility of being His disciple. Great growth and transformation happens with general faith. Reading the Bible and trusting it is working in our lives without a specific faith goal in mind does produce great growth. Just worshiping God, or giving or serving, also do great works in our soul, whether we consciously believe for it to happen or not. But there are regular times God wants you and me to exercise specific faith; where it is necessary for progress to be made. That is why He so often gave people promises before they happened.

God could have just given Abraham a son without saying anything about it to him. Most of us have not been told by God in advance we would have a child, it just happens. But God told Abraham over twenty years before Isaac was born that he and Sarah would have a child. Why did God do that with Abraham? He wanted Abraham to learn to believe so that he could become. A lesson God wants us to learn as well.

So how does this work in adding Christian virtues? Let's say you are struggling with this goodness thing. Maybe you grew up in a mean spirited home and being good is hard for you. You are being faithful in your devotions and trying to do you part, but you still have these regular bouts of meanness. You know this is something

Section III—The Process

God is dealing with at this time, so how do you add goodness to your life? First, admit to God that you need His help. Second, look at Scriptures on God's goodness, love, etc., and then take the concrete step of believing God to add it to your life. Pray and say something like, "Father, You are good. Your word says that you desire me to add goodness to my life. I am looking to You and making a decision to believe You are going to add Your goodness to me. I am believing so that I may become, just as You said." When you start to pray that way and believe God to do it, He works as only He can in your life. You are putting the "pressure," if you will, not on you to make yourself good but on God, who has the power and willingness to do it. From this base, you can and should take practical steps and look for ways to practice goodness in your daily life; but it is still done with your trust and focus in God to develop this in you. This can work in any area of your life that needs "adding to," as you follow God's lead.

The first time I saw this work was in the life of a missionary I know. This man has such love coming from him there is no doubt it is from God. Everyone who is around him feels loved and encouraged. When Janet and I mentioned that to his wife, she told us that several years earlier he felt God challenging him to walk in a higher degree of love. So every day for over a year, he read 1 Corinthians 13 which is called the love chapter because it describes godly love in a clear and powerful way. He would read it and pray it and believed God to increase or add godly love to him. It sure worked. His wife said wherever they went, people commented on the love of God that flowed out of him. Remember the bald spot in my yard and that bald spot in my soul? As I practice sowing God's word and believing

Chapter 2 • Receiving from God

God to do it, He is filling in the barrenness with fruitfulness.

Let me finish this chapter with a biblical "watch out," followed by the most powerful word you can ever say to God. Hebrews 4:1–2 (New King James Version) says, "Therefore, since a promise remains of entering His rest, let us fear lest any of you seem to have come short of it. For indeed the gospel was preached to us as well as to them; but the word which they heard did not profit them, not being mixed with faith in those who heard it." God's word, His seed, carries His life in it and is capable of doing everything He sends it to do. It is, however, possible for these life-giving, power-packed words to have little or no effect in our lives if we do not mix them correctly with the key ingredient. Remember, there are hundreds of types of breads, but they all have some key ingredients, which must be mixed together for it to be called bread. If they stay separate (flour, water, yeast, etc.), they never become bread. For God's words to work in our lives, those words need to be mixed with faith in our hearts. Those Exodus Jews heard God's words but did not receive them. They did not mix them with faith and consequently those God words did not profit or help them. The writer of Hebrews is telling us that negative consequence is also possible for us, too, if we do not receive God's words. It is not a given that God's wonderful words will produce in our individual lives, they have to be mixed with faith. How do we do that? By saying the most powerful word you could ever say to God—Yes.

Let's picture the seed of God's word coming your way (by reading it or hearing it), landing on the soil of your heart. You have a choice to make. If you say, "No, that is not true, I can't believe that, I won't receive it," the soil is hardened and the seed just sits there. If, however, you say,

Section III—The Process

"Yes, God, I receive your words, I embrace them, I say yes to them," your heart receives that seed, it is mixed with faith and begins to do a God work in your life. This is the rest that the writer of Hebrews talks about later in the chapter; it is the rest of faith that leads to obedience and changed responses. The German translation here is great, "Glaubensgehorsam," which combines the two words "faith" and "obedience" into one, literally meaning "faith-obedience." Real faith will lead to obedience and changed actions; it is the natural outgrowth. This brings such rest to your soul. You are putting your faith in God and His word, not in your human ability to make it happen. You trust, then practice and obey God's directives, and watch Him do what you could never do on your own. It's a wonderful way to live.

Every time I say yes to God's words, God's will, I open the soil of my heart up to Him, and His powerful, imperishable, divine seed goes into my heart and begins to work. Realize, when a seed grows, it fills space that once was something else. Two objects cannot fill one spot; something has to move. God's word, His seed, begins to grow and expand, and that seed begins filling the soil, spreading out, increasing, and pushing through the soil, and then breaks through the unseen underground into the visible dimension above ground. As it continues to grow, it fills space once occupied by air as it presses upward. In a similar fashion, as we believe God and trust Him to work, His word pushes aside dirt and emptiness, and fills our souls and lives with godly traits and blessings. A God tree grows and it produces much beautiful and satisfying fruit. He does what we could never do.

You have to remember though, like a seed, the results generally do not happen overnight. They take time. Faith

Chapter 2 • Receiving from God

and patience, endurance and perseverance, are needed, and that is what we will look at next.

Chapter 3
Dealing with Delays

I do not like delays. No, let me restate that: I hate delays. I especially hate delays due to traffic. I do not know what it is, but sports and traffic bring out some of my absolute worst responses. In my mind, there is absolutely nothing good about sitting in a traffic jam. I do manage to pray for a while, but then I start thinking about how I could pray better somewhere else. Then I think about how I could be using my time so much better if I were not stuck here. Why don't these people learn to drive? Don't they know I am the most important person on the road and they should all get out of the way and let me go where I'm going? It is almost a heavenly experience for me when the lights are green and I get through one after another. I love early morning or late evening drives when there are very few cars or trucks getting in my way. Nope, I just do not like aggravating traffic jams and delays.

Chapter 3 • Dealing with Delays

What is especially true of me when driving is true of most of us regarding the delays of life; we do not like them. If we really do not care much about an issue, or if we are not in a lot of pain, or if it is a non-essential, it is so much easier to deal peacefully with delay. We can be so patient and understanding in these circumstances. "Sure, go ahead in front of me. I'm in no hurry. Have a wonderful day!" If, however, the issue is important to us, delays can be agonizing. "When is it ever going to happen? Lord, why is this taking so long?" Yet delays are an unavoidable part of life and something, it seems, that God really wants us to learn to deal with. In almost every list of Christian virtues found in the New Testament, there will be some reference to patience, perseverance, or endurance. "And let endurance have its perfect result, so that you may be perfect and complete, lacking in nothing." (James 1:4 NASB) I love those results; being mature, perfect, complete, and lacking in nothing, sound great. I do not like having to endure to get there. So, I either have to learn to deal with delay or else I am going to live a very frustrated, griping, "acting like a baby" life. My family has seen just that in me, the mature teacher of God's word, leader of leaders, in traffic jams. How about you?

There is a consistent pattern in Scripture of God's dealings with people. It goes like this:

1. God gives a person a promise before it happens.
2. The person decides what they are going to do with that promise.
    a. They say, "Yes, Lord," and the promise is planted like a seed in their heart and life.
    b. Or they say "No," and the seed of the promise sits on top of a hardened heart, easy to be stolen

Section III—The Process

       or blown away.
3. If the person says yes, that yes is followed by a period of time: a delay, a testing, or spiritual resistance of some type.
4. Along the way, during this delay time, the person has more decisions to make that are very important and part of God's growth program.
   a. Keep hanging on to the promise, even though it looks like it is not going to happen.
   b. Completely give up, saying, "This will never happen. I quit."
   c. Go through some doubting times, possibly even quitting for a while, but then repenting and going back to the promise and saying yes to it.
5. If the person hangs in there, in time, the promise is realized.

There are many examples of this in Scripture, but for the sake of time and space let me mention just a few. Joseph was given a dream (a word or promise) by God that he would become a great ruler. His brothers got so mad at him for his prideful dreaming that they sold him into slavery and he was carted off to a foreign country (Egypt). He made the most of this time, serving His master faithfully. His reward was to be falsely accused of attempted adultery by his master's wife and to be thrown into prison. Instead of the promise being realized, it went from bad to worse. A time of testing, of delay, of unfair circumstances was his experience. At this point, how easy it would have been to get mad at God and just quit? This went on for years, not just days or months. Then, when Joseph interprets a dream correctly, Pharaoh appoints him to be his right hand man in the most powerful country in the world at the time. It really

Chapter 3 • Dealing with Delays

is like a movie with a happy ending, except this is no fictional tale, it actually happened.

Moses had the dream of seeing his Jewish brothers free, rather than living as slaves in Egypt. He tried to get things rolling in his own strength, killing an Egyptian to help a slave. He had to flee into the desert and spent forty years in isolation living as a simple shepherd. I'm sure he thought his dream would never come to pass; he had resigned himself to living a comfortable but unfulfilling life in the desert. Then God showed up in the burning bush. Moses gave every excuse he could think of as to why he was not the man to bring Israel out of slavery, but God did not listen to his excuses. God said, "You're the man." Moses had a decision to make. Receive God's words and go for it, or tell God no. We know he said yes, but when Moses went to Pharaoh, as God instructed him, things got worse for the Israelites rather than better. He did what God said, but, at first, circumstances got worse. Moses had to make another decision after God told him He was about to do some really big things in this situation. He could believe God and keep going, or quit and go back to the old life. Thankfully, he decided to keep on believing, and God then did some of the greatest miracles in history in bringing Israel out of slavery and into the Promised Land. God fulfilled His word, but He worked with and through Moses to do it.

This type of pattern is recorded in the life of just about every positive Bible role model: King David, Daniel, Isaiah, Abraham, Isaac, Jacob, Peter, and Paul. It will be true of you and me too. As uncomfortable, and sometimes painful, going through this process can be, it is one that is important to God and invaluable to us. Thankfully, this process will not be necessary in every area of our lives, but it will be in some. If we realize it and understand our role,

Section III—The Process

we can "consider it all joy" (James 1:2) when we face these times and let them do what they're intended to.

What is God doing through these times of delay? Two main works: 1) He is preparing us for our future by building and developing authentic faith, character, and skills, and 2) He is working the garbage out of our souls.

First, let's look at preparation and faith development. 1 Peter 1:6–7 (The Message) says, "I know how great this makes you feel, even though you have to put up with every kind of aggravation in the meantime. Pure gold put in the fire comes out of it proved pure; genuine faith put through this suffering comes out proved genuine. When Jesus wraps this all up, it's your faith, not your gold, that God will have on display as evidence of his victory."

Richard Wurmbrandt once told the story of a Christian being persecuted for his faith. A communist official was mocking the Christian saying, "Where is your God in all this suffering? Christianity is just a crutch for the weak." The Christian responded, "A bridge is not tested with the weight of a matchstick, anything can hold a light weight. It is only genuine and strong when it can carry the weight of a train. Genuineness is only proven through pressure and weight. My faith is in God and will hold up under anything. What is your faith in?" Our brothers and sisters in persecuted countries know this reality firsthand and are examples to us here in the United States. Faith delays, prayers that we keep looking to be answered, and working through adversity, are some of the main ways for genuine, authentic, better than gold faith to be developed. If it is always easy, real faith and character cannot be developed.

Plants that have a small or shallow root system can easily be uprooted, but trees with a deep, strong root system can withstand incredible storms. Muscles grow stronger

Chapter 3 • Dealing with Delays

through lifting and moving weights of some type. If a muscle is not used, it atrophies and grows weaker. After I broke my arm, it was placed in a cast for six weeks. When the cast was removed, I was shocked at how much hair now covered my arm, how small it had gotten, and how much it smelled. Through lack of use and lack of resistance, my arm had gotten so weak. Faith and character that does not go through pressure, weight, and delays will be an ugly, hairy, weak, smelly faith. That is not God's way. He is a God of excellence who is developing gold, Christ-like character in us.

In this process, we will go through the "I wonder if this is really working," and "I wonder if God is going to come through" tests before we can become oaks of righteousness instead of weeds of wimpiness. We've looked briefly at Joseph's life earlier in this chapter, now let's see what God says was going on and why.

Psalm 105:18–21 (NASB) says this about Joseph's testing time, "They afflicted his feet with fetters, He himself (His soul came into) was laid in irons; until the time that his word came to pass, the word of the Lord tested (refined) him. The king sent and released him, the ruler of peoples, and set him free. He made him lord of his house and ruler over all his possessions." Remember, Joseph had gotten a dream and word from God. Then He was tested and refined by God's word as he went through harsh conditions and seasons of delay until the time came that His word came to pass. This is the type of testing we all go through at some point; God makes a promise real to us and we receive it by faith. Then we need to keep on believing it and standing on it through contrary times until God's time comes and the promise is fulfilled. Like Joseph, God will bring us into the

Section III—The Process

place of ruling over greater areas of our life; areas He has ordained for us.

During seasons of delay when we deal with thoughts such as, "When am I ever going to become a peaceful person? Am I ever going to become a person of courage or self-discipline? Is this really working? I do not see anything changing. It's been so long," it is important to realize what is happening, because continuing to believe is important for the fulfillment of some promises. Galatians 6:7–9 (NIV) says, "Do not be deceived: God cannot be mocked. A man reaps what he sows. The one who sows to please his sinful nature, from that nature will reap destruction; the one who sows to please the Spirit, from the Spirit will reap eternal life. Let us not become weary in doing good, for at the proper time we will reap a harvest if we do not give up." When we are in this waiting time (after sowing to the Spirit, sowing God's word in our hearts and in our lives), then we have to watch out for possible deception. The deception is this, "I'm not going to reap what I sow." Because there is that season of waiting, where it appears that nothing is happening, when in reality it is, it frequently happens that people are deceived and lose what God wants to do. Our response here is very important. We have to learn to strengthen ourselves so that we do not let weariness set in. God tells us clearly, if we do not give up, if we keep on doing right, keep on trusting God, "at the proper time" we will reap a harvest. I know, the "proper time" is almost always later than what we want, but God really does know best and He will come through.

If our responses were not important during this waiting time, there would not be so many Scriptural encouragements and admonitions to keep on doing good, to persevere, and to keep on believing. Hebrews 6:11–12 (NASB)

Chapter 3 • Dealing with Delays

states it clearly, "And we desire that each one of you show the same diligence so as to realize the full assurance of hope until the end, so that you will not be sluggish, but imitators of those who through faith and patience inherit the promises." It is by continuing to believe, enduring, and exercising patient faith that we inherit what God has promised. This does not mean that if you've ever had a second or minutes or even days of wondering if it's really going to happen that you've short-circuited the whole process. It does mean you have to work through those questions and doubts and settle it your heart again that "God is faithful to His words. His words are like a seed that is growing and it will produce at the right time. My part is to trust and obey, God will do the rest."

In time, if we stay with it, the seasons of doubt will get much shorter and easier to defeat. When Abraham first started his journey with God, he needed lots of external confirmation but he still had some major failures. Later in his life, though, he had grown and developed to such a degree that when God gave him one of the greatest faith challenges in history, he did not fight it or resist it or doubt it one bit. He believed God could even raise his son from the dead if needed to fulfill His promise. In time, that can happen with us as well. We can become those whose normal response is trusting faith, people who can fairly easily shrug off the doubts.

If it takes longer than what we think it should, the temptation is very real to get lazy or sluggish. That is why the writer of Hebrews encourages us to be diligent and to watch out for "sluggishness." If you have watched sports for any length of time, you've seen this with teams. If a team keeps losing, it is hard for them to keep giving it their best, not to get sluggish, because they have lost hope that

Section III—The Process

things will ever change. When successful coaches are asked how they turned around a losing program, they almost always say, "We had to change their mindset. We had to get them to start believing that they could win and believe in the system." Losing, lack of results, and delay can cause laziness and sluggishness, but when we refocus and change our mindset, believing in God and His system, we start winning. If we can get and maintain victory in our hearts, it is just a matter of time until it starts happening in our lives. So realize what is happening, encourage yourself with this understanding to stay with it, and look at the examples of people who endured until the answer came, until the change happened. This is how you partner with God in the times of delay.

The second main reason for these testing times is to work the junk out of our souls. Even if a container is filled all the way to the top with some type of liquid, none of it will ever spill over until the container is moved, shaken, or turned over. The same is true with us. We can have a lot of anger, fear, or pride inside of us that can remain well hidden if everything is going our way, going smoothly. But when things start to shake, when pressure is applied, when the heat is turned up, when it is not going how we want it to when we want it to happen, what is inside us will come out. Me getting angry with traffic jams shows that I still have some of that inside me. When a person shrinks back in fear when faced with adversity, it shows a deposit of fear is still inside them. Because our responses do matter, God uses life to make us aware of these garbage bags of the soul. He does not do it to condemn us, remember there is no condemnation for those who are in Christ, and not to make us feel horrible about ourselves. He does it so we can realize

Chapter 3 • Dealing with Delays

what still needs to be worked on and so we will come to Him for grace and help.

Jesus said the mouth speaks from that which fills the heart. Listening to yourself, especially in pressure situations, tells you a lot about the condition of your soul. James tells us that real faith will have corresponding works. You and I can say we believe something, but until our actions match our thoughts and words, that belief is not yet at a mature level of development in our lives. What is in me will eventually come out. If I have sown to the sinful nature, I will at some point, reap a sin harvest. When that harvest is seen by me, it helps me realize what types of seeds have been sown, so I can, in God's power, deal with them. This is crucial for life change and that is what we're going to look at in the next chapter.

Chapter 4
Dealing with Our Enemy's Schemes

A few years ago, a young woman came to my wife wanting some Christian advice and prayer. She was a bubbly, cheerful person who was a joy to be around and was growing well in her newfound relationship with Jesus, but she had an unusual problem. At different times throughout the day she was regularly, and literally, pulling her hair out. She had been doing it for years and did not know why she did it or how to stop. To cover it up she tried different hairstyles because, from time to time, people would comment on those unusual looking areas in her hair. She did not want to do it and often did not realize it was happening until after she did. Janet talked with her, prayed with her that one time, and she never did it again. Pulling out her hair came to a complete stop. Yea God!

There is probably a psychological diagnosis for her condition that could possibly have been helped through

Chapter 4 • Dealing with Our Enemy's Schemes

counseling and therapy, but God got rid of this condition for her with a little talking and a short prayer. You would think everyone would be happy for this young woman and would give God thanks and glory for doing it, recognizing God does indeed answer prayer. However, the way Janet prayed would give some people cause for concern. The reason being, that she prayed specifically against a spiritual force, against Satan's power and influence.

I know many Americans, even Christians, do not think there really is such a being as the devil. They think he is some sort of legendary creature, or symbol of darkness, which came to be as the result of primitive people trying to explain the evil they saw around them. Yet Jesus, God in the flesh, who had perfect understanding and perfect spiritual perception, dealt specifically with Satan and his forces on a regular basis. Jesus attributed much of the suffering in this world directly to Satan. For example, Jesus said Satan tries to tempt us to do evil (Matthew 4:1–11). He causes physical, emotional, spiritual, and social torment (Matthew 4:24, 8:16, 8:23–34). Jesus and other biblical writers call him a murderer, thief, accuser, destroyer, deceiver, liar, and more.

When the New Testament is read with an open mind, it is clear that Jesus dealt on a regular basis specifically with Satan and his servants. It continues through Acts, through the rest of the New Testament, and into church history. There can be absolutely no doubt about it, Jesus and His personally- trained followers all believed in and dealt with the devil and his forces.

Yet, today, in many American churches, the power of Satan is hardly ever, if ever, taught. There are several reasons:

Section III—The Process

1. With the Enlightenment and the acceptance of modernism as the predominant worldview, anything supernatural, anything that could not be visibly and scientifically proven, was suspect. On the one hand, this brought about some great developments. It replaced many superstitious and nonbiblical views and practices with research, practical explanations, and incredible advancements in so many fields. However, as modernism is now being replaced by post-modernism, it is clear the scientific method did not come up with all the answers (otherwise it would not be replaced). Nevertheless, modernism was the predominant worldview, at least in the West, and fostered the view that belief in anything supernatural was silly or non-existent.
2. Extremes in the church are another reason for avoiding this subject. Throughout church history, when a biblical truth has been rediscovered, it is rarely in a balanced form. Almost always, prophetic voices have extremist tendencies. When the church, in the twentieth century, began to rediscover the charismatic gifts, supernatural ministry, and deliverance from demonic power, it was carried, by some, to an extreme. Some ministers and sincere believers were casting demons out of everything that moved. They acted as if everything was a demonic problem and all a person had to do to get rid of that problem was to rebuke the devil.

   Biblically discerning people were taken back and appalled by this extreme view and practice. Obviously, many problems were not demonic. Instead, they were issues of spiritual and personal growth; learning to handle money wisely, learning how to

Chapter 4 • Dealing with Our Enemy's Schemes

communicate with others, or how to deal properly with conflict, for example. People not wanting to be associated with extreme practices then put a valid and helpful biblical practice out of the church, or at least into the back room. Many churches which taught the Bible as God's inerrant word basically ignored this aspect of Christian belief and ministry. In reality, many churches had the view, "Yes, in theory we believe there is a devil, but his main works are in darkest Africa, not in civilized America."

3. The church rightly wants to reach the lost in a highly educated, civilized society. Talking about devils and demons runs a major risk of closing people off to the message of Christ because so many consider them silly or nonexistent. Since reaching the lost is of primary importance, some have decided to talk about such issues rarely, if at all.

4. Some churches believe and teach that because God is sovereign, everything that happens in this world is God's will. They believe Satan may tempt us a little, but he really cannot do anything to us. God is in control, so everything that happens, all suffering, all sickness, all torment, and all abuse, is His will. We just need to yield to all of it because it is the work of a God who loves us, and whose ways are beyond our comprehension.

These are some of the main reasons the evil one is ignored in many American churches today. I certainly understand those reasons, and I was hesitant about including this chapter because I do not want to overemphasize Satan or close the minds of seekers to the message of Christ. I do

Section III—The Process

believe that God is sovereign and all-powerful, and I certainly appreciate logic, sound reasoning, and the scientific method. I do believe the majority of our problems and issues do not specifically need to address the devil in order to get victory over them. We should not live our lives focused on the devil. We should live Jesus-focused lives. Yet, there are many people who are struggling with issues that counseling, medicine, spiritual disciplines, or accountability partners alone, cannot adequately aid. Some areas will not be changed until a spiritual force of darkness is dealt with.

Luke 13 tells of a time when Jesus was teaching in a Synagogue on a Sabbath day. A woman who had a physical problem for over eighteen years came to Jesus for healing. Jesus laid His hands on her and did, in fact, heal her. The religious leaders in the synagogue got upset with Him for healing on the Sabbath, a day of rest. This woman should have been healed on another day, not the Sabbath, they said. Jesus then pointed out their hypocrisy with a great response in verse 16 (NASB). He said, "And this woman, a daughter of Abraham as she is, whom Satan has bound for eighteen long years, should she not have been released from this bond on the Sabbath day?" Did you see that? Jesus, the Son of God, said that Satan, a spiritual power, had bound this woman all these years. It was not God who did it, it was Satan and Jesus came to destroy the works of the devil (Acts 10:38, 1 John 3:8). Jesus said she needed to be "released from this bond," giving a mental picture of someone bound up with perhaps a rope or a chain. When Jesus laid hands on her and spoke to her, He released her from this spiritual bondage that had kept her in physical pain for such a long time. She could have prayed more, read the Bible more, gone to church more, and surrendered to God

Chapter 4 • Dealing with Our Enemy's Schemes

more, but she would never have been released without dealing with the true source of this condition.

Are all sicknesses directly from Satan? Does the devil always need to be addressed when praying for a person to get better physically, emotionally, or mentally? No, but sometimes he does. How the enemy gets a hold in our lives, how to recognize it, and how to deal with it is what we'll briefly cover in the rest of this chapter. There are some excellent books that deal with this more fully, but this will give you a good start.

Let's start with some key concepts:

1. Satan wants to use us and destroy us. He hates God, but since He can do nothing directly to Him, he attacks God's children.
2. Satan is not all-powerful or omnipresent. He is powerful compared to us, but is nothing compared to God.
3. There are different levels of demonic activity in people's lives. Temptation is something we all face. If we continually yield to it, it can become a "stronghold" that is tough to break, but can be broken with Jesus' power. Relatively speaking, possession rarely occurs and almost always involves occult practices and/or deep sin or severe abuse. Satan cannot just jump on someone and possess them. He does try to tempt all of us though.
4. Satan's main strategy is to steal God's word from our hearts and replace it with his words. Please read (#4) that first sentence again. In the parable of the seed and the sower (Matthew 13:19–23), which we've talked about several times, Jesus said God's word is God's seed. The soil is the human heart, the

Section III—The Process

>inner man. Jesus then gives three types of attacks the enemy uses to either steal the word from us or to make it unfruitful. Jesus said the enemy first tries to make the soil of our hearts hard, so the word will not penetrate it at all and he can easily come and steal it away from us. This occurs mainly through wrong beliefs, a lack of understanding, disappointment with God, or pride. Once again, if no word is received, there is no God-seed and therefore no eternal life in a person's inner man. If that approach does not work, then Satan brings heavy-duty pressure with persecution, accusation, and/or adversity, to try and make the word unproductive in us. We could call it the fire hose method. If that attack does not work, then he tries a gradual, slow choke method. If we do not actively guard our hearts then, Jesus said, life's worries, riches and pleasures can actually choke God's word so that it does not mature. When this happens we stay stuck as spiritual babies, never becoming all God has planned. As you can see, Satan's goal is to steal God's word or make it unproductive in us. If we realize this, we have grasped his main strategy for ruining our lives.

Our enemy not only tries to steal God's word from our hearts, he also tries to plant his own seed, his words and experiences. In Matthew 13:38b–39a (NIV), after He explains the parable of the sower, Jesus talks about tares and wheat. In enlightening His disciples on the meaning of this parable, Jesus says, "the tares are the sons of the evil one; and the enemy who sowed them is the devil." Although He is describing why God lets evil people continue to live with His people on His planet (His field), Jesus makes it very

Chapter 4 • Dealing with Our Enemy's Schemes

clear that the devil also sows and plants. He sows people who will do evil and he tries to sow his lies in people's minds. From the very beginning, he got Adam and Eve to believe his words rather than God's. When they believed the devil's words, his seeds, they quickly responded in rebellion and distrust towards God. Death soon followed, as it always does. Even with Jesus Himself, the devil tried to get Jesus to receive his words and reject God's. Jesus realized what was going on and used the very words Satan tried to replace to defeat him. Jesus knew that just as God's seed produces godliness, the devil's words produce eventual destruction.

If the enemy can get us to believe and receive his words, thoughts, ideas, and experiences rather than God's, then he has gained a major foothold from which he can spread more darkness in our souls. Seeds do grow in fertile soil and our hearts have tremendous potential for growing a strong and large harvest. Have no doubt about it, the words we receive as truth will grow in their influence, for good or evil, unless we do something to stop them. The type of results we eventually see depends upon the type of seeds that are sown and watered.

How do we deal with the enemy's seeds and trees (strongholds) in our lives? There are three main ways, to do this, with the first being the absolute best way to get rid of destructive seeds/words/thoughts/ideas. What is this very best way? Stop them before they are ever planted. Do not let them grow any roots at all in your mind and heart. Most spiritual warfare does not involve specifically naming or fighting against the devil. It is much more about receiving God's love and truth, and living a God-connected life. If we are soaking ourselves in God's presence and truth, then anytime the enemy's lies are heard, we can fairly easily

Section III—The Process

shrug them off as idiotic or throw them off with just a little effort. Evangelist Reinhard Bonnke has said, "Flies do not sit on a hot oven." If we live spiritually focused, "on fire," living God's truth type of lives, most of the enemy's attacks will fail because those "flies" have nowhere to land.

When national magazine articles come out, as they do every year, telling us why we cannot believe the Bible, or that Jesus is not really who the Bible says He is, I shrug those words off easily. Why? Because I know God's word is true. I know what God's word says about Jesus and I've seen that the redundant arguments or latest discoveries are always full of huge holes. Those words, or seeds, gain no entrance into my heart at all. When I am constantly filling myself with God's words, I keep being filled with the Spirit and keep living for God. Consequently, my heart is soft and fertile for God, and hard against the enemy. Giving him no access at all is the very best way to defeat Satan's schemes.

If, however, we have entertained the devil's words for a while (and we have all done that to some degree), and we have let them into our hearts and minds, then we need to take more direct and strong action; the second approach to dealing with the schemes of the devil. When I was in high school, the first *Exorcist* movie came out. I cannot tell you how many of my big, strong, aggressive football player friends had trouble sleeping; wondering if the devil could just jump into them and take over their lives. We all felt pretty helpless; wondering that if there was such a thing as the devil, what could we do to stop him from taking control of us? One of my friends, a big man, could not sleep at night, thinking the devil or his demons were in the closet. But the enemy cannot just take our lives uninvited; we have to open the door. The main ways we open the door are: 1) through occult involvement, 2) through repeated sin in a

Chapter 4 • Dealing with Our Enemy's Schemes

specific area, 3) through a tragic, hurtful experience in life (rape, abuse, death of a loved one, etc.), 4) through sins in our family tree (problems and tendencies that run in our families), and 5) by receiving the devil's words over God's words.

If any of these things have happened, it is possible that the enemy has gained a degree of influence in one's life. At this point, it is often necessary for one to repent, renounce, and then resist the devil's words, experiences, or influence. James 4:7 (NIV) says, "Submit yourselves, then, to God. Resist the devil, and he will flee from you." Since most of the time we are the ones who allowed him to gain influence, we need to say, "God I am sorry for allowing this in my life. I repent from it. I turn from it. I renounce its influence in my life and tell it to go in Jesus name." Some strongholds occur because of other people's wrongdoing to us, which does not require us to ask God to forgive us. We move on to realizing the stronghold, and renouncing and resisting it. Either way, it helps to be specific.

For example, if you have received fear of the future in your soul, then specifically renounce it and tell it to go. This does not mean you are possessed, it simply means the enemy has had influence in part of your life. In Luke 10:19 (NIV) Jesus said, "I have given you authority to trample on snakes and scorpions and to overcome all the power of the enemy; nothing will harm you." Jesus said He has given His followers the authority to draw on His power by using His name to overcome every attack of the enemy (Mark 16:19). When we resist the enemy in Jesus name, with His truth, the enemy has to go. Jesus is so much stronger than anything the enemy can throw against us. We can have confidence that when we get to the root of our problem,

Section III—The Process

turn from it, renounce it, and resist its influence in our lives, the spiritual aspect of our problem will be broken.

Especially at this point, it is then extremely important to soak yourself in God's truth on that subject. Scriptures such as 2 Timothy 1:7, which says, "God has not given you a spirit of fear, but of love, power, and a sound mind" and others are good. It helps to personalize them by saying Scriptures in this way, "Since God is with me, I will not be afraid. God is watching over me more than the sparrows. He will take care of me" (Hebrews 13:5–6, Matthew 6:26–27). This then helps us fight the enemy's lies because as Ephesians 6:11 tells us, God's word is like a sword that destroys the enemy's strongholds. Therefore, we break the lie and replace it with liberating truth.

That brings us to the third way to deal with the devil's schemes. If a spiritually negative trait or influence has been part of our life for a long time, even with the immediate release we get by repenting, renouncing, and resisting, it can take some time before a new way of responding becomes natural for us. I have seen many people who recognized the enemy's lie and have renounced it in Jesus name, but wondered what was wrong when they did not immediately act much differently. Sometimes there is an immediate, dramatic change, but often it still takes time to build in new responses. Several winters ago, an ice storm tore up a tree in my front yard. A friend and I cut up and hauled away the remains of that tree, but it still took some time to fill in the spot where it once stood. Today, you would have no idea a tree was ever there, but for a while you could see some of the remaining secondary roots and the hole it left. If we uproot a large tree, a major stronghold in our lives, it takes some time to fill the soil in and grow a new one. The same is true of our souls.

Chapter 4 • Dealing with Our Enemy's Schemes

In the parable of the sower, Jesus said the person who ended up experiencing good and lasting results was the person who held on to God's words and, over time, with perseverance (there's that word again), bore great fruit. A Christian does not have to fear the devil because Jesus has given us authority over him in our areas of influence. However, we do need to be aware and watchful because Satan is a wily foe with thousands of years of experience in dealing with human beings. 1 John 4:4 tells us the One in us, Jesus, is far greater than he who is in the world. Jesus defeated Satan in every way possible and now, through Jesus, we too can defeat his schemes and increasingly walk in God's life and victory. Instead of us pulling our hair out, we can leave the devil pulling out his.

Section IV—The Practices

Chapter I
Changing through Prayer

    The summer after my sophomore year in high school, one of the football coaches instituted a weight lifting program for anyone who wanted to participate. I enjoyed football, but had a problem common to many teenage boys; I was too skinny. Because I could run pretty fast and was too dumb not to back away from smashing into people bigger than me, I had made the varsity team as a sophomore and played quite a bit even though I only weighed one hundred and forty pounds. By that next summer, I had added fifteen pounds through natural growth, but I realized that I needed as much strength as I could get, so I signed up for this program.
    My coach was a great man who really knew what he was doing. He was a strong leader, knew how to push you, and still keep it fun. I had never lifted weights before, so I did not know what to expect. My coach showed us the rou-

Section IV—The Practices

tine he wanted us to follow and showed us how to lift the weights correctly. I remember the first time I did a bench press; all I could manage was one hundred pounds for just a few repetitions. It was not a very impressive beginning. At the time, I did not realize it would be good to do an in-season weight-training program to maintain off-season gains, so I just lifted weights during the summers over the next few years (I played other sports the rest of the year). Once I got to college, I began to lift weights throughout the year and have continued since then.

From that initial day of weight lifting to the beginning of my college football days, in a little over two years, I put on twenty-five pounds of mainly muscle. In that amount of time, my bench press tripled. Weighing one hundred and eighty pounds, I bench-pressed over three hundred pounds and increased in all the other exercises anywhere from 100 to 400 percent, depending on the exercise. These types of gains are not at all unusual for those who stick with it, and some people see far greater increases. I was sold on weight training as a way to grow muscle and gain strength.

There are different theories on the best way to lift weights to maximize results, but they are all built on some basic principles. Stress the muscle through resistance, let it rest to recuperate, stress it again, let it recuperate …you get the idea. The weight has to be heavy enough to stress the muscle (doing lots of repetitions with one ounce will not build strength), then there has to be enough time to let the muscle recover and build back up before it is stressed again. No weight lifter can keep doing maximum bench presses every day and keep increasing their strength; the amount of weight they can lift will actually decrease if they lift too often. Weights act as a stimulus that causes the muscles to respond and grow stronger.

Chapter 1 • Changing through Prayer

What does this have to do with spiritual growth and transformation? There are some practices and some spiritual disciplines, which we can all learn to do that will help us partner with God to grow and change. They will help stimulate growth and help us reach levels of development that are not possible otherwise. There is no way I could have ever increased my strength by 100 to 400 percent without doing a good strength program. There is no way we can grow and become all God intends us to be without engaging in the spiritual practices and disciplines Scripture tells us about. As the philosopher Dallas Willard said, "To live the way Jesus lived; we must do what Jesus did." Jesus modeled for us the principles and practices we can all follow to help us be and do all God has planned.

As we have repeatedly talked about in this book, our focus is on God to help us change. The person of Jesus, the power and leading of the Holy Spirit, God's words, His truth, and faith in Him, are what help us break through barriers and go on to a level of fruitfulness that we could never reach on our own. In other words, it is God Himself, His presence, which is the greatest force for change in the life of a human being. When God enters a situation, something is going to change.

Romans 4:18 tells us that because Abraham believed what God promised him, he became what God said he would become; believing led to becoming. Verse 17 (NASB) gives us a very important insight into this process, "(as it is written, 'A father of many nations have I made you') in the presence of Him whom he believed, even God, who gives life to the dead and calls into being that which does not exist." Again we see God gave a promise before it ever happened and even described it in past tense language; "a father of many nations *have* I made you." From God's

Section IV—The Practices

perspective, when He declares something, it is a done deal. He has absolutely no doubt that His word has the power to do what He sent it to do. God is a God who has resurrection power, He can bring the dead back to life and He brings things into our realm of reality that were not previously there. Abraham was able to exercise such exemplary faith because he received that promise while in God's presence, "in the presence of Him whom he believed." In the presence of the living God, faith soars and the miraculous becomes believable. It is God's presence that makes everything else come to life.

His presence is the greatest gift, the greatest honor, the greatest blessing that God could ever give us. That is why the most famous Bible heroes made having His presence with them, or being in His presence, their number one request and goal. In Exodus 33, God told Moses that He would send His angel to be with the people of Israel to bring them into the Promised Land, but that because of Israel's continued stubbornness and rebellion, He would not personally be with them. Moses then says to God, "If your presence does not go with us, do not send us from here. How will anyone know that you are pleased with me and with your people unless you go with us? What else will distinguish me and your people from all the other people on the face of the earth?" (15–16, NIV) Moses understood it was only God's presence that distinguishes us from all others on this planet. It is only His presence that makes us able. It is only God's presence that makes real life possible. So Moses said, "Angels are great, but that is not enough. Unless you go with us, we do not want to go." King David echoed those same sentiments when he said, "One thing I ask of the Lord, this is what I seek: that I may dwell in the house of the Lord all the days of my life, to gaze upon the

Chapter I • Changing through Prayer

beauty of the Lord and to seek him in his temple." (Psalm 27:4 NIV) David did not mean he literally wanted to do nothing but sit in a temple building his whole life (he was definitely a man of action); what he did mean was that the presence of God was his greatest longing. God Himself is the ultimate reward; being in His presence is the greatest honor.

Paul continues this theme when he writes, "But whatever was to my profit I now consider loss for the sake of Christ. What is more, I consider everything a loss compared to the surpassing greatness of knowing Christ Jesus my Lord, for whose sake I have lost all things and consider them rubbish, that I may gain Christ" (Philippians 3:7–8 NIV). Paul, who had seen miracle after miracle, and who had seen entire cities change because of his powerful ministry, said knowing Jesus was so awesome that everything else was simply garbage in comparison. Throughout history, those who know God best all echo that sentiment. This theme is woven all through Scripture; the presence of the Lord is the greatest reward, the greatest experience, the greatest lifestyle, and the greatest power for change in existence.

So how do we experience God's presence? If I had to answer that question in one statement it would be: We experience God's presence on a regular basis by learning to live in the attitude and practice of prayer. Prayer is something that is practiced by almost every theistic religion under the sun. The longing for God has been woven into us by our Creator, and prayer is both a main way by which we express that longing, and a means by which we encounter the God who put it in us. God does not want to be an occasional visitor in our lives; He wants to be involved with us all the time. That is why Scriptures like 1 Thessalonians

Section IV—The Practices

5:17 encourage us to "pray continually, pray without ceasing, pray all the time" (NIV, NASB, The Message), because living a lifestyle of prayer is the way we learn to live in God's life-giving presence.

The attitude and the practice of prayer are key words to remember. The attitude of prayer refers to an openness, awareness, and hunger for God. Unfortunately, it is possible to pray, to say the words, and to do the practices without focusing on God. That is not biblical prayer. The practices of prayer would be understood as actually engaging in the various types of prayer the Bible describes. Some people say they never really get alone with God and pray because they live in an attitude of prayer. Jesus demonstrated for us that both are important if we want to live in God's presence.

Jesus said He would never leave us or forsake us (Matthew 28:20, Hebrews 13:5–6). On great days He is with us, on boring days He is there. When we have done well, He celebrates with us and when we have done something terrible, He is still there to help us back up. Yet, there are far too many Christ-followers who rarely experience His reality because they have not practiced His presence on a regular basis. I, like many others, have read and been inspired by the classic book, *Practicing the Presence of God*. This book is a compilation of letters written by a monk, named Brother Lawrence, several hundred years ago. This humble man continues to bless countless lives with the insights he shared with friends about how he learned to practice God's presence no matter what he was doing. Over the years, he grew in prayer to such a degree that he was constantly aware of God's presence with him and learned to live in the grace and joy that can only come from God. Whether he was alone in his room, or washing the dishes, or working

Chapter 1 • Changing through Prayer

on some other task, he learned to live in God's presence. He would practice throughout the day turning his thoughts and heart towards God in prayers of different types, attitude, and practices.

I love the word practice because it means we are learning. It is ok to make mistakes as it is not yet the game itself where there is more pressure to be perfect. In practice, when someone messes up and starts getting down on himself, other players, or the coach may say, "Shake it off, it's only practice. This is what practice is for." Even after thirty years of following Christ, I do not live constantly in an attitude of prayer, but I continue to practice and get better at it year after year.

When I used to read the phrase, "pray without ceasing," I wondered how in the world that was humanly possible. I thought prayer only meant getting in a room alone with God or in a corporate setting with other believers, doing some type of praise and worship, and then making requests of God for a while. On top of that, I read biographies of famous Christians and some of them wrote about spending hours and hours each day in prayer. So many times when I would pray, I would pray everything I could think of and look at the clock to find that only ten minutes had passed (maybe up to thirty minutes if I sang a lot). I did not see how I could ever live life that way. Then I saw in the Bible, and heard from more experienced teachers, that there are all types of ways to pray. Worship, praise, and singing psalms are refreshing, God-pleasing ways to pray. Reading the Bible, meditating on Scripture, even studying with an awareness of God's presence are also ways of "continually praying." Sitting in silence before God, reflecting on a situation, listening to God, asking God to intervene in a person's life or a situation, and proclaiming His inspired word over a

Section IV—The Practices

situation are some other ways to pray. And they all count! There are many ways to pray and the Bible encourages us to use all of them at the appropriate times (Ephesians 6:18).

Learning to live in God's presence through a lifestyle of prayer is our goal. Even though sitting in a room strictly praying for hours each day may not be everyone's grace, the practice of prayer is necessary for each of us to live in God's power. Jesus, God in the flesh, modeled both the attitude and practice of prayer. He prayed early in the morning, He prayed throughout the day, He prayed at night, sometimes even throughout the night. Luke tells us that even in the middle of ministering to crowds of people, Jesus would take prayer breaks to get alone with God (Luke 5:15-16). Jesus was certainly living with an awareness of the Father's presence with Him, so why did He take time to get alone with God? Because He knew there are some things that happen, and need to happen, only in the practice of prayer. That is why Jesus said, "But when you pray, go into your room, close the door and pray to your Father, who is unseen. Then your Father, who sees what is done in secret will reward you" (Matthew 6:6–7 NIV). Jesus knew that He needed to have time with God where He shut the door to everything else going on and met with Him in private so He could live in the reward or power God wanted Him to have. Jesus knew that we need to do this as well. If we want to learn to live in God's presence all day, if we want to hear His voice in the noise and crowds of everyday life, we need to learn to experience His presence and hear His voice in the quiet of one-on-one times with Him. It is impossible to learn to live in His presence, in a lifestyle of prayer, without the regular practice of prayer.

Let's look briefly at some of the different ways to pray, and how it helps us in the transformation process.

Chapter I • Changing through Prayer

Praise and worship. Psalm 22:3 (NASB) says, "Yet, You are holy, O You who are enthroned upon (inhabit) the praises of Israel." People like Pastor Jack Hayford have written extensively on this subject, but to summarize briefly, God comes into a situation where people are praising and worshiping Him from their hearts. God's presence is always with us, but it can intensify. Many of us experimented with a magnifying glass as children. We saw first hand the power of intensifying the suns rays by holding a magnifying glass where the sun's rays could hit it, and then we'd watch as things caught on fire (let's not comment on some of the objects we burned). The same sun that was always there, its presence, was intensified in a specific situation through the magnifying glass. Heartfelt praise and worship welcome God's presence into a situation with a deeper level of intensity and power. That is why, so often in Scripture, from the walls of Jericho coming down (Joshua 6), to a prison being shaken apart (Acts 16:25–26), that acts of power were preceded by praise and worship. Praise and worship opens us up to God and helps us experience Him in unique ways. It certainly counts as a central part of prayer.

Fellowship with God. "We proclaim to you what we have seen and heard, so that you also may have fellowship with us. And our fellowship is with the Father and with His Son, Jesus Christ" 1 John 1:3 (NIV). May I encourage you to make worship and fellowship with God the foundations of your prayer life? Christianity is relational. God designed it to be that way. John wrote that he and those first disciples had fellowship with the Father and the Son and then with others. Fellowship means the sharing of life; close friend-

Section IV—The Practices

ships and deep relationships. There are all types of ways to have fellowship; doing an enjoyable activity together, having free-flowing conversation, sharing a meal, and even working on something together. The main focus of fellowship is time with that person or those people. Even though God is invisible to our natural eyes, He is Spirit, God has still given us the capacity to have fellowship with Him. We remind ourselves He is here and we consciously focus on Him being with us. When we do that, we can have fellowship with God through reading the Bible, sitting and being still, conversation in our heart, worship, or any of the other types of prayer.

If we get away from fellowship, prayer will quickly turn into a formula, list, duty, or purely forced discipline. That makes prayer something we have to endure or force ourselves to do, rather than the life producing practice God wants it to be. Shifting worship and fellowship away from the beginning and center of prayer is one of the main reasons too many Christians avoid it. When asked about their prayer life, most respond, "I know I should pray more, but I have trouble doing it." They do not understand the many different ways to pray, or they have let it become a "make myself" commitment, rather than alone time with the greatest, most loving, joy-filled, pure Person ever. The devil and the sin nature have to be dealt with because they certainly try to hinder our desire to pray, but it should not be a forced obligation, a battle every time you think of prayer. Other types of prayer should also include the fellowship element, but unless we keep fellowship first, the other practices of prayer can take over and in the end, will make prayer a duty rather than a joy. Keep fellowship first.

Chapter I • Changing through Prayer

Intercession. Ezekiel 22:30 (NIV) says, "I looked for a man among them who would build up the wall and stand before me in the gap on behalf of the land so I would not have to destroy it, but I found none." In intercession, we enter into the labor of prayer. In intercession, we draw on the Spirit's power and leading to pray God's will into a situation ("build up the wall") and as God's representatives on earth, ask for His mercy, love, and power in a situation. In the Ezekiel passage, God said he was looking for an intercessor, but because he could not find one, He was going to have to pour out judgment rather than mercy. This is a huge topic, but God honors the prayers of His people so much that, if He can find people to intercede, He can stop or greatly reduce the judgment people's sins have earned them. Abraham interceded for Sodom and Gomorrah and, as a result, the one righteous man in those cities was spared, along with his daughters. Moses interceded for the people of Israel. Jesus intercedes for us now in heaven, and God uses the intercessory prayer of His people today to change the world.

How does that help us experience God and change us? As we pray for others in this way, we get to know God's heart and actions in a way that is unique. We were not designed to focus mainly on ourselves, so when we start interceding for others and for situations God has placed on our hearts, the river of the Spirit flows. Rather than being clogged up by selfishness, we labor with God in prayer to help others. When we give time, energy, and effort on behalf of others, God loves to bless it. So often, when in intercessory prayer, I have God experiences that I do not get in other ways. Sometimes, I actually feel a little bit of God's love for people, or a little of the burden of His heart, or get an understanding of Scripture, or even gain direction

Section IV—The Practices

for my own life as I intercede for others. The biblical meaning for the word "know" often means an experiential knowledge, not just mental. When we work with someone, we get to know them in a different way than just socializing. We see their expertise and their skills, perhaps their passion comes out as they do meaningful work. The same happens when we intercede: we get to know God in this aspect of His being, it rubs off on us, and His Spirit works in us.

Intercession can lead us into "spiritual warfare," as described in Ephesians 6:12, 19 (NIV). "For our struggle is not against flesh and blood, but against the rulers, against the authorities, against the powers of this dark world and against the spiritual forces of evil in the heavenly realms. With this in mind, be alert and always keep on praying for all the saints." Sometimes as we pray, the Holy Spirit will make clear to us that the devil is attacking someone or a situation, and He wants us to pray against it. It can be a spiritual attack that involves emotions, health, finances, or any other area of life. One time Janet felt a sense of urgency to pray for her father. We began praying in the Spirit and felt led to pray specifically for her father's protection and against the devil's attack. Later, Janet found out that at the exact time we were praying, her father was in a serious accident in which his truck went down a steep embankment and he was thrown from the vehicle at a high speed. He just happened to land in a bush and was fine. That was an attack of the enemy, which the Lord let us know about and God used our prayers for his protection. God will use you in that way as well, and when you fight together with someone (God), you become close in a special way. Just ask soldiers who were all strangers on the first day of basic training, but

Chapter 1 • Changing through Prayer

ended up forming life long friendships and bonds because of the struggles and battles they went through together.

Petition. Petition is the most well known type of prayer. It is simply asking God to meet a need—ours, or someone else's. Jesus called it asking for "our daily bread." He encourages us to talk to God about all our needs and to ask Him to meet those needs in the appropriate way. When we talk to God about concerns, we open our hearts to Him. He is the best friend we could ever have, so He will take those concerns to heart. As we ask Him to help, He will get involved in the appropriate way. He will often deal with root issues by challenging us to greater faith or to take an action, but other times He will give us peace and He will handle it. If we bring our requests to God, not just praying mindless words or repetitive phrases, we invite God into that situation and He will work as only He can.

While there are others forms of prayer, these are some of the main ones that help us experience God's presence and thus produce positive change. In the next chapters, we are going to look at a few more prayer practices that have been particularly helpful to me and others in partnering with God for life change.

Chapter 2
Prayer Planning

A church where I previously served, completed a large building campaign. A large atrium, a five-hundred seat chapel for medium-sized events and services, a youth center, new classrooms, a connecting walkway, plus extra parking and new landscaping have totally changed the appearance of the church and helped ministry be done better. It was a tough project for the contractor and the builders because they had to retrofit new buildings to the existing structures. From time to time, I would walk around the construction area and be amazed at how they made it all fit together so well. There is so much involved in making something like that happen; so many things that have to be done just right for it to work. They did it though. They put all the pieces together and it looks great.

As important as execution was in completing this project, none of it would even have gotten off the ground

Chapter 2 • Prayer Planning

without a well-thought-out plan. Without a clear plan, no one would have been able to do anything, because to start a building project you must first know what it will look like when completed. The end product determines the materials, finances, workers, and steps needed to complete it. No big project can be started, let alone completed, without a plan.

Just as a plan is needed to complete physical buildings, a plan is also needed for spiritual growth and transformation. Spiritual growth and change is a big, God-ordained project that will last, at least, our lifetime. It is a God-project with eternal consequences, yet many believers just "leave it to God" as to how it will happen. I agree that our trust is in God to complete what He has started in our lives, and that God is always working at a level we are not even aware of. He is the One carrying the heavy load of making His purposes come to pass in the world and in our lives. However, He wants us prayerfully seeking as to what His plan is and what our part in it should be, because, as has been stated many times in this book, He works through us and with us in accomplishing His purposes.

For the first years of my involvement in ministry, we intentionally kept planning to a minimum. In response to a fresh outpouring of the Holy Spirit where many traditional practices were challenged or bypassed, quite a few of us overreacted when it came to careful planning. Many churches were spiritually sick or dead, with little of God's life changing power present. Some of this was due to over-planning and organizing. Absolutely everything was planned and organized to such a degree, that even without God's presence, they could run their programs. We were young, on fire, and thought we just needed God to show up and everything would be great. We went overboard in the opposite direction. We often quoted verses like Isaiah 30:1

Section IV—The Practices

(NIV), "Woe to the obstinate children," declares the Lord, "to those who carry out plans that are not mine, forming an alliance, but not by my Spirit, heaping sin upon sin," and Proverbs 3:5 (NIV), "Trust in the Lord with all your heart and lean not on your own understanding." We kept planning to an absolute minimum because we wanted to be led by the Holy Spirit; we did not want to design plans that were not from God, and we did not want to trust in our human reasoning.

This may shock some of you, but I remember many times meeting with our worship team right before the service, praying for a while, and then just going out to see what would happen. We did not know what songs were going to be sung. Often, I did not even know what I was going to speak on, until I got to the pulpit. Amazingly, many times it worked: God showed up, the worship was great, the message spoke to people, and an impact was made on the members of our congregation. As we grew, however, we saw that to make sure that ministry happened during the service we really did need to do some planning. Children's ministry had to be set up and organized; you cannot just let small children roam around and expect them to receive ministry. The same went for their parents. Small groups needed to be organized so people would have relationships and growth experiences that do not happen in a larger service. Ushers, greeters, sound people, communication systems, and so much more, had to be set up so ministry could happen. We gradually began to see planning was necessary and even godly when done prayerfully.

God is a planner. He does things on purpose, for a reason, with a goal in mind. One of the most encouraging and quoted Scriptures in the Bible is, "For I know the plans I have for you," declares the Lord, "plans to prosper you and

Chapter 2 • Prayer Planning

not to harm you, plans to give you hope and a future." (Jeremiah 29:11) God is not haphazardly getting out of bed each morning, stretching, yawning, and then saying, "Let's see, what do I feel like doing today? Maybe I'll send revival to Nigeria and judge Libya. No, wait a minute, let's reverse that. No, I don't feel like doing that either. It seems like a Costa Rica day to Me." Thankfully, God is not like the god's of Greek and Roman mythology who did act that way. From Genesis to Revelation, the Bible makes the point that God has plans and purposes that He is working to bring to pass. He has purposes for countries, for people groups, for times, and seasons, as well as for our own lives. Rick Warren's *Purpose Driven Life* has become one of the most purchased books in history because it struck a chord with people. What chord did it strike? What is its message? God has a purpose for your life and it is found in Jesus. It is true that God is working out well-designed, well thought out plans, and He wants to reveal at least some of them to us, so we can cooperate with Him.

What are God's big purposes? Some of them are preparing a people to rule and reign with Jesus, to fill the earth with His glory, to reach people from every people group with the gospel, and to form Christ in each and every believer. If we get clear on the big purposes, it gives us a clear compass reading on which way to head. God is brilliant and powerful enough that He has ordained specific, unique plans for each of us to help in accomplishing the bigger purposes. He does have an individual plan for each of us, but it will be in harmony with the big goals He has set for the earth and for eternity. If we look at where God is heading and then make prayerful plans to head in that same direction, it makes God's grace much more available for transformation.

Section IV—The Practices

Okay, so God has plans, isn't that enough? Should you really plan, especially for spiritual growth? You can see planning practical aspects of life (education, finances, work, etc.), but spiritual growth? I would say you especially need to make plans for spiritual growth, because significant spiritual growth rarely just happens. It has to be intentional on our part. God is working in our lives in a masterful way, no doubt about it, but there are so many things He wants us to be a part of actively. He wants us to know the joy of accomplishment; he wants us to aim at an important target and hit it, not just let life happen to us.

God is raising sons and daughters to maturity. He is preparing His people to rule and reign with Christ, and that takes a lot of preparation and training. Part of the growth process is learning to hear what God is doing, then doing our part in seeing it happen. In Matthew 25, along with several other stories He told, Jesus made clear that managing what God has given us is essential for growth and change. He told about a business owner who went on a long trip, leaving certain amounts of his assets to some of his managers (called "stewards" in the story). Each manager was given the right amount of assets to work with, according to their ability, until the business owner came back. After a long time, the owner came back, got his three managers together, and heard their reports on what they had done with what he had given them to work with. The two who took what was entrusted to them by the business owner and had used it to gain more, received great praise and increased influence from their boss. The manager who was lazy and did nothing with his boss's assets actually had those assets and his position taken away from him. Jesus said this is one aspect of how God's kingdom works and how God will respond to us. He carefully chose what assets

Chapter 2 • Prayer Planning

we should have to fulfill His purposes in the world, and He expects us to work with them and make a difference with them. He wants us to take what He has entrusted to us and to do something positive with it, to increase it. In order to do that, in order to manage what He has given us, we must prayerfully plan.

The answer to making our own false plans is not to do no planning, the answer is to prayerfully plan; to seek God's guidance and to wisely think through the areas of life over which He has given us responsibility. Have no doubt about it, we will each stand before God and give account of what we did with what He entrusted to us. He put a great deal of thought and effort into giving us the right gifts, abilities, and resources to make a difference in the world, and He gives us grace, His Spirit, His word, and the right people to make it happen. So let's make the most of what he has given us. Let's prayerfully plan what it is He wants us focusing on. When we do that, His power will be available to make it happen.

How do we plan prayerfully? Different people have different approaches, but one I have found most helpful is to list the various areas of life God has entrusted to me, and then to seek His guidance as to what He wants me to focus on in those areas. There may be a few who hear so often and so clearly from God that they do not need to do this, but in my experience they are a very small minority. If God clearly speaks to someone to do something, no matter what it is or when God asks, they need to do what He says. For most of us, there are significant time periods between those major, dramatic, clear words. We can still discern God's will by taking some practical steps for knowing His plans at the time.

My list, as I mentioned above, goes like this:

Section IV—The Practices

1. Relationship with God
2. Personal Development
3. Marriage
4. Family
5. Work
6. Church
7. Mission in the World

Your list may be a little different, but those are my main areas of responsibility and my main priorities. Depending on the season of life I am in, certain ones will be emphasized more than others.

American author, salesperson, and motivational speaker, Zig Ziglar, often draws a circle with each of these areas being like a spoke on a wheel. God is always at the center with the spokes extending outward. Each of the spokes needs to be in balance for the wheel to roll smoothly. Each area, each spoke, needs to be developed, but not all equally or at the same time. In fact, it is just about impossible to make major changes in all these areas at once. Over time though, each area can and should be grown and developed.

Some people are so good at this that they live every day based on their priorities and specific purposes. They are generally very disciplined and focused, and reach more specific goals than those who are not. I think it is great for everyone to develop this ability; after all, self-control is one of the fruits of the Spirit. I am not sure, however, if being that specific and detailed regarding each day works for everyone. For some people, looking over their priorities and goals each and every day, making a list and checking off each item, would be more of a burden than an inspiration. I used to think everyone needed to function this way, but

Chapter 2 • Prayer Planning

over the years, I have seen some very productive people who seem to function better without such an orderly approach. I am somewhere in between these two types. At the very least, no matter what type person you are, being clear on where you are headed and why you are headed there is important. Keeping in your mind what God wants you to focus on is helpful for everyone. It is hard to know if you have hit the target if you do not have one.

How does it work? Let's take priority number one, relationship with God, and work with it a little. I generally take some time to "prayer plan" big goals once a year, and then review them every four months or so (some people do them quarterly or every six months). I pray, saying, "Lord, what do you want me to focus on in my relationship with you this year (quarter or month)? Then I get quiet, or pray in the Spirit, for a while. Sometimes, and I love it when this happens, a real clear, no doubt about it, God-thought comes into my mind: "Mark, I want you to focus on getting rooted and grounded in My love." When those clear words from God come, they are generally pretty brief and to the point (at least with me). If I get that, I do not have to pray much more about it because God has clearly spoken to me. If that does not come, and for me, most of the time it does not, I then begin to reflect on my relationship with God by asking myself (in an attitude of prayer) some questions like, "How is my time with Him? How are my feelings towards God right now? Is my heart on fire for Him or is it lukewarm or cold? What am I wondering about God right now?" Asking questions like this has proven very beneficial to me. When I think through questions like that, I find it helpful to write my thoughts down. Then over the next few weeks, I reflect more on those questions with a prayerful attitude. Even in prayer, I get all kinds of thoughts depending on the day and the time. Some thoughts get me very excited right then, so I am tempted to receive that as God's final word to me. However, over the years, I have seen some exciting thoughts that were not always from God. On the other hand, some other thoughts that went through my mind without a whole lot of fanfare ended up being from Him. I think, especially on bigger and longer-term goals, it is like sifting through dirt to get to the gold. As I reflect and pray, some of my ideas and thoughts lose their appeal in my soul and others increase. After a few weeks, I generally have a peace about which of those ideas are from God and I then write them down.

After receiving clarity on what I should focus on, I next write down some possible action steps to help me get to where I want to go. What steps can I take to get rooted and grounded in God's love? I could, for example, study Scriptures about God's love and goodness and meditate on them. I could look at barriers in my life to God's love, such as negative experiences, disappointments, thoughts, and beliefs. I could read books or listen to teachings by others who have gotten some real insight into God's love. You get the point.

I then go through those different areas, using the same process until I have peace that I am focusing on what God wants me to. Some people like to sit down and do it all at once. Others cover one a day or one a month. It does take some time to do this, but it really is worth it. It helps you say "yes" to the right things and "no" to all those other things, even good things, you could be doing. I believe the big question we need to ask ourselves to be in peace, as well as to keep pressing on, is, "Am I doing what God wants me to do right now?" If I am doing what He wants, that really is all that matters. Everything else is going to

Chapter 2 • Prayer Planning

pass away or get burned up anyway. If you have never gone through this process before, be careful not to write down too many goals or plans. It is very easy, once you start prayerfully considering the goals God would have you set, to start thinking of many different possibilities. One thought easily leads to another. Get rooted in God's love. Yes, love is the greatest virtue for any human being. Faith is big too. Yes, I'm going to make growing in strong faith one of my main goals. That leads to hope. Yes, I need hope, after all that is the starting point for specific faith. Hope only works with knowledge of the truth, so I had better commit myself to memorizing a chapter a day out of the Bible. Before you know it, you have five wonderful goals just in that one category, but I guarantee you that you will not be able to do all those at once, in addition to the other areas God is going to have you focus on. If you try to do more than what God is giving you grace for, you will not be able to do it. At that point, you may be tempted to give up on the whole thing and just passively let life happen, or you may feel condemned because you have not been able to do everything you want to right now.

I once read an interview with management expert Peter Drucker and he encouraged leaders to have two, maximum three, major goals over a six-month period. He said more than that is really not possible to do well. I think that is true of personal growth and development, too. Write down one, maybe two, goals for each category and then prioritize those goals down to two or three major ones. You can still give some attention to the others, but for specific desired change to occur (remember God is always doing more than we are), discipline yourself to keeping the number of goals down to just a few at a time.

Section IV—The Practices

After going through this process, review it and make adjustments as needed throughout the year. Sometimes, despite sifting through ideas, I focus on a goal that really should be for later (I am not perfect in this), or other times I have reached that goal and can now move on to another, or I learn of another way to help me get where I need to be. I do find it helpful to read over those goals and action steps on a regular basis to keep them fresh in my mind and to keep me on target. That leads us to the next prayer practice that will help us grow and change.

Chapter 3
Prayer Pictures

My grandfather was an amazing man. Growing up on a farm in southern Illinois, he had to become the man of the house at a very early age. Partly out of necessity and partly out of aptitude, he became skilled in many practical areas. He built the house my mom grew up in and that home is still occupied today, over eighty years after he built it. During World War II, when things were scarce for most people, he built a tractor from spare parts. I have friends today who have that same ability. They just have a knack for knowing what to do to put something together or make something work.

I am amazed at people like that because I seem to have landed at the far left side of the bell curve in such matters. It does not seem fair to me that just a generation stands between my grandfather and me, yet I got hardly any of that aptitude. I could tell you stories, and my wife could tell you

Section IV—The Practices

even more stories, of my attempts to be a handy man; and how many times we ended up having to call someone who knew what they were doing. I guess the one good thing about it is that she does not ask me to do as many handy things anymore, given my record.

When putting something together, if there is going to be any chance at all that it turns out right, people like me have to follow written instructions. With my limitations, I know I must have directions and follow them at all times. In most cases now, the directions include not only written steps, but also pictures of the items. Diagrams are shown of how something should look as it is being put together, and ultimately what it will look like when completed. For people like me, the more angles shown, and the fuller the description, the better off I am.

Written words and visual pictures compliment each other and help us understand and function better in most areas of life, including spiritual growth and transformation. The next couple of chapters are going to look at some of the most helpful ways I know to help faith come alive and grow strong as we cooperate with the Holy Spirit to change our responses and actions and ultimately grow to be more like Jesus. The first is to use prayer pictures.

When I say prayer pictures, I do not mean having little colored pictures of Bible stories in your room or stashed away in your Bible. I do mean getting a picture in your mind of what the Bible is describing with a prayerful attitude. According to Bible scholars Fee and Stuart, the Old Testament is 40 percent narrative, and much of the New Testament is in story form as well. Stories help to paint a picture in our minds, and pictures help the story become real to us. The more real something becomes to us, the

Chapter 3 • Prayer Pictures

more impact it has on us. That is why God gives us physical and mental pictures as tools for transformation.

Genesis 15:5–6 (NASB) says, "And He took him outside and said, 'Now look toward the heavens, and count the stars, if you are able to count them.' And He said to him, 'So shall your descendants be.' Then he believed the Lord; and He reckoned it to him as righteousness." When God gave Abraham the promise that he would be the father of many nations, he could have just given him spoken words. He did do that, but along with the spoken words He took him outside and gave him a physical picture; one that he could carry in his heart and mind. Why did God do that? Why didn't He just give him words? After all, hearing a clearly spoken word from God is an incredibly powerful experience. I think the reason God gave him a picture as well, is because of the powerful effect pictures have on our beliefs and then on our actions.

A clear mental picture always precedes every great work of architecture, every great invention, and every great accomplishment. At one point in time, these works did not exist in our world. Then someone got an idea and put that idea on paper, or in a computer, as words and/or a drawing. That picture was both a goal and a faith expression: this dream will come to pass. Our faith, our responses, play an important role in the fulfillment of many of God's promises, so God gives words and pictures to help our faith be strong and for our responses to be on target.

Spiritually speaking, most of us have the same basic lack of aptitude that I have in doing handyman-type things. We have real trouble understanding what God is like, how He works, and what He is doing. The Bible describes sinful man as spiritually blind and dead, incapable of seeing correctly or producing spiritual life without being converted.

Section IV—The Practices

Jesus said, "no one can see the kingdom of God unless he is born again" (John 3:3b NIV). Once we are born again, born of His Spirit, we then gain the capacity to begin to see spiritual truth, see how life works, see what God is like and more. We do not see it all perfectly in this life, but we sure see it a lot better than when we were spiritually blind.

We talked earlier about changing the set of our minds in order to flow in the Spirit's power. We have talked about how in certain instances believing is the key to becoming. We have talked about getting God's plan and getting some direction as to what He is working on during the various seasons of our lives. Getting a biblical, truth-based picture of God's promises and His goals for us is a huge help in enhancing all of these things. In my mind, if I can see myself becoming what God desires, it does help me think, believe, and start acting that way. Psychologists tell us it is impossible for a person to act consistently in a way other than how they see themselves. If I see myself as a loser, I will eventually, and consistently, act like a loser. If I see myself as being loved by God, I will eventually, and consistently, act like someone loved by God. It is how God designed us.

The first time I heard about this practice was in the early '80s. Paul Yongi Cho (now David), pastor of the world's largest church and a man I greatly admire, wrote about how, once he started picturing the answers to his prayers and picturing what God wanted to do through his ministry, it began happening in amazing ways. His church started in a Seoul ghetto right after the Korean War. From extreme poverty, in a primarily Buddhist nation, he built a local church of approximately eight hundred thousand members (just in that one church), and started thousands of others. I read how he waited for God to give him a clear

Chapter 3 • Prayer Pictures

word or promise, then he prayed until he got assurance in his heart that it was done. Next, he began picturing the answer and he saw tremendous results.

After reading that, plus the biblical examples he gave of the language of the Holy Spirit being "visions and dreams," as described in Acts 2 and other places, I also began to practice this. I started visualizing the church I felt God wanted me to lead. I visualized a church of thousands, and then tens of thousands, turning Germany upside down for Christ. I started visualizing every good thing I could think of, setting my faith for those things to happen. Yet, after years of doing that, plus everything else I could think of to help, it never did happen. The church I led grew into the hundreds, but it never did make it into the thousands. Years later, hardly any of the things I was picturing and believing for actually happened. Many of my pastor friends had the same experience. Even today, some twenty-plus years later, there are no churches with thousands of believing members in Munich. Does that mean the principle is not valid? Should we not use mental pictures as a means of praying effectively and becoming what God wants us to become?

I do not doubt it has worked for Dr. Cho and for many others, and I still think it is a valid practice. Athletes use this practice when getting ready to compete or perform, and studies have shown it does enhance performance. Speakers and actors have often used it to improve their work. I do not think there is any doubt that it is a sound, even Biblical, practice. So why didn't picturing my desired future work for me in church work? I'll give you my opinion.

You have probably heard the phrase, "If you can see it, you can become it. If you can see it, you can have it." I think that is correct. If it is really God's will and His time, if we have received a promise from God, then picturing it

Section IV—The Practices

will help our faith connect with it, and help it come to pass. Even non-Christians set goals and use mental pictures to help them succeed. However, I do not think it works nearly as well if I just come up with an idea that I want God to make happen. I know God wants to reach many people, but maybe our church in Munich having thousands of members was not His will at that time. Maybe I was not able to manage it well enough, maybe the season for Munich's harvest has not yet come. I do not know for sure. I do not know for sure what God's exact plans for you are either. However, this I do know, God is working in each and every one of us to form us into the image of His Son. We can certainly take His promises, be led by His Spirit, and begin to picture ourselves becoming the way God describes us as His bornagain, Spirit-recreated people. We can take His words and begin to see ourselves filled with His love. We can imagine love being poured into our hearts from our heavenly Father and flowing through every part of our souls. We can picture ourselves loving our spouses and children and then every person with whom we come in contact with. As we continue to practice prayerfully, seeing ourselves that way, we will begin to believe that way and then act that way.

We are visual creatures, and what we see and look at will determine, to a great degree, the direction we go. My wife regularly encourages me to keep my eyes on the road because I have a tendency to look at things while driving when I see something interesting. The problem is I do not want to stop and look; I want to look while driving. For some reason, Janet gets concerned when I am not paying as close attention to what is going on with other vehicles around me as she thinks I should. Sure, the car veers a little, but I stay pretty much on the road. I still do not understand why women get upset at such things. The point is, it

Chapter 3 • Prayer Pictures

is almost impossible to look at something in one direction while you go in another. We follow what we see. That is the power of prayerful mental pictures. The thing I am focusing on, picturing, seeing, will determine, to a great degree, the direction I go in life.

I am not sure exactly how it works, but words themselves can become pictures in our minds. Paul wrote, "You foolish Galatians, who has bewitched you, before whose eyes Jesus Christ was publicly portrayed as crucified?" (Galatians 3:1 NIV) Paul said the Galatians got a portrait, a picture, of Jesus' death, and what it accomplished. How did they get it? Through Paul's speaking and teaching, he painted a picture for them using spoken words. You may have heard the illustration, if I say the word "elephant," in your mind you do not think of the letters e-l-e-p-h-a-n-t. Instead, in your mind, you see the massive creature with the long trunk, big ears, and trumpet call. Words can become pictures, which make it real to us.

Revelation 4:2–5 (NIV) says, "At once I was in the Spirit, and there before me was a throne in heaven with someone sitting on it. And the one who sat there had the appearance of jasper and carnelian. A rainbow, resembling an emerald, encircled the throne. Surrounding the throne were twenty-four other thrones, and seated on them were twenty-four elders. They were dressed in white and had crowns of gold on their heads. From the throne came flashes of lightening, rumblings and peals of thunder. Before the throne, seven lamps were blazing. These are the seven spirits of God. Also before the throne there was what looked like a sea of glass, clear as crystal." Why does Jesus give us this description of the throne area in heaven? There are certainly spiritual truths to be learned, but along with learning truth, there is the point of helping us "see" the

Section IV—The Practices

spiritual realm better. When we take these God-given words and meditate on them, which can include picturing them, the Holy Spirit takes them and helps make it more real to us. It is real, but until it becomes real to us, it does not have an impact us.

One time when I was meditating on the above passage, it hit me how colorful God and heaven are. I looked up the different colors listed in this passage and realized that, too often, I saw God in black and white, rather than color. When I was a child, we had a black and white television for years. I loved it when we went to people's homes that had a color television. It was so cool to see colors on the screen rather than just black, white, and gray. As I pictured this scene in heaven, it hit me in a fresh way how the very atmosphere around God is filled with life, color, beauty, and powerful activity. I had a deeper experience with God because I saw Him in a fresh way, and it happened as I pictured what the Bible described.

The same happens with us when we meditate on, or picture, who God says we are. God says we are more than conquerors through Jesus. Do we see ourselves facing every obstacle in life and getting through it better than we were before we faced it? God says Jesus has set us free from the yoke of sin and the Law. Do we picture ourselves as being free, defeating sin, living in the grace and life of the Holy Spirit? God says He has put His joy in us. Do we see ourselves "rejoicing always" as a lifestyle? Do we see ourselves living each day with a smile on our faces, rejoicing in God even when challenges and hardships come? If we practice picturing ourselves the way God says we are, if we picture the goals He has given us coming to pass, over time we will see those things increase in our lives.

Chapter 3 • Prayer Pictures

When God wanted to help strengthen Abraham's faith, he gave him a picture. Let scriptural pictures fill your mind, too, and they will help your faith grow strong and your thinking and actions will begin to follow what you see.

Chapter 4
Prayer Proclamations

Like many Europeans, the entire time we were in Europe, we lived in an apartment. The cost of housing in larger cities can be outrageous, so a large segment of the population never owns a home; they stay in apartments. When we moved back to the United States, prices were so much cheaper that we were able to purchase our first home. It was early November when we moved in, so we quickly needed to use the heat. When I turned the heat switch on, nothing happened; no heat came out of the vents. I went down in the basement where the furnace was and quickly saw there was no activity there whatsoever. The large machine was cold and dead. Since where we lived in Europe used steam heat that was provided for the whole building, I had never before dealt with an American furnace. I was really hoping nothing was wrong with it, since we had just had the house inspected and were assured it was fine. I

Chapter 4 • Prayer Proclamations

went across the street and asked a neighbor if he had any idea what to do. He came over, looked at it, and said, "You need to light the pilot light." We looked at the directions on the furnace (it helps to read and follow the manufacturer's directions) and lit it. Even after lighting the pilot light, there was still just a little, tiny flame burning in this large machine, and no heat was being produced. From the basement, my neighbor yelled up to Janet on the ground floor to turn the thermostat up. When she did something powerful happened. Jets of fire began blazing and blasting through the furnace with great intensity and energy. For a furnace novice like me, it looked so cool seeing those powerful flames come to life! In just a few minutes, the entire house was at a comfortable temperature as the furnace pushed heat to every room.

I believe when we receive Jesus as our Lord and Savior, we connect with God as our fuel source and the pilot light in our inner man is lit. The Holy Spirit places God's fire, God's life, inside us where before it was dead and cold. Yet even though God's Spirit now lives in us, and we have the potential for being powerful furnaces for God, we need to know how to turn on and turn up our spiritual thermostat. Prayer proclamations are one of the best ways I know to kick the flames on so that Holy Spirit's power, energy, and heat is released in our lives. Ephesians 5:18–20 (NIV) says, "Do not get drunk on wine, which leads to debauchery. Instead, be filled with the Spirit. Speak to one another with psalms, hymns and spiritual songs. Sing and make music in your heart to the Lord, always giving thanks to God the Father for everything, in the name of our Lord Jesus Christ." When God says to be filled with the Spirit, it means for this to happen in a continuous, ongoing manner, not as just a one-time experience. We need the fire of the Holy Spirit

Section IV—The Practices

flowing through us every day of our lives if we are going to live God's way. When we do what this passage tells us and speak to one another, sing, and give thanks, which are all verbal expressions, God fills us with His life changing presence on a continual basis. We do not have to live at a minimal, pilot light level.

Spoken or sung words can be the result of being filled with the Spirit. In the book of Acts, each time there is a passage describing people being filled with the Holy Spirit, there was always a verbal expression such as spiritual language (tongues), prophecy, preaching or all of them. There were other results as well such as boldness, miracles, great love, faith, etc., but every time a verbal response is recorded as happening (Acts 2, 4, 8, 10, 19), Jesus said the heart speaks from what fills it. So it makes sense, if we are full of the Spirit, Spirit words will come out of our mouths.

However, words are not just the result of the Spirit's work; they are also one of the best ways to fill our hearts with God's presence and to transform our lives. James 3 gives three descriptions of the effect of spoken words: 1) words are like the bridle in the mouth of a horse, 2) words are like the rudder of a ship, and 3) words are like a fire in a forest. Each of these illustrations shows us, if we want to change our direction or be energized, words will play a big role in it. We know that even though a horse is much larger and stronger than its rider is, the rider can control the direction of the horse by turning the bridle, which is in the mouth of the horse. Even though ships can be enormous, the captain can guide the ship where he wants it to go by turning the rudder. A forest can be huge, covering hundreds of square miles, but one little fire can burn up much, or all, of it. All three of these examples indicate the tongue, though very small, can change things much larger than it.

Chapter 4 • Prayer Proclamations

James uses the words "turn, steered, course" in describing the power of words. God has set it up in such a way, that if we want to change our course, we need to change our words.

Romans 10:9–10 (NASB) says, "that if you confess with your mouth Jesus as Lord, and believe in your heart that God raised Him from the dead, you will be saved; for with the heart a person believes, resulting in righteousness, and with the mouth he confesses, resulting in salvation." This connection between faith in the heart and the spoken word is made often in Scripture. The passage above tells us how it works when God grants us salvation: we believe, which results in us being made righteous in God's sight, and we confess, which results in salvation. Speaking words, in faith, based on God's word, seals and even releases tremendous salvation and transformation blessings. When a person believes in Jesus and then says it with his mouth, it changes the direction or course of their life. Faith in the heart and words in the mouth are a powerful combination.

Notice in Romans 10:9, "confess" comes before "believe." In verse 10, "believe" comes before "confess." This shows that it can flow both ways. 2 Corinthians 4:13 (NASB) says, "But having the same spirit of faith, according to what is written, 'I believed and therefore I spoke,' we also believe, therefore we speak." If we believe what God says, our words will be in line with Him. If I believe Jesus is God's Son, I will say it. On the other hand, if I want faith to increase in my life, speaking, confessing, or proclaiming it will cause it to grow stronger inside me. Years ago, John Wesley asked one of the Moravian church leaders how to get the faith he was talking about. This leader told Wesley to "preach it until you get it." In other

Section IV—The Practices

words, proclaiming God's truth with a hungry heart will cause faith and fire to grow stronger in our inner man.

In my own life, when I make prayer proclamations of God's word, or based on God's promises, it does a powerful work in my soul. Many times, when I have trouble getting energized for the day, I take time to speak or sing God's words about who He is, who He has made me to be, or what He is going to do, and the fuel of the Spirit flows over that little pilot light and kicks on a whole new dimension of faith and energy. Every person who has ever spoken, preached, or taught God's word knows, just as the Moravian leader told Wesley, how a person can literally preach himself happy. At our church, I regularly try to give people with speaking gifts opportunities to use that gift. Ninety-nine percent of the time, after speaking, they have a glow of joy on their faces. There are several reasons for that: 1) they have given to others and giving releases receiving, 2) they are using gifts God has given them, which brings fulfillment, 3) they normally get some encouraging feedback, and encouragement lifts everyone, and 4) they have spoken God's words and those words have caused the fire to increase inside them.

I know this practice of faith proclamations (or positive confessions) has been abused and/or exaggerated. Some have tried to use it for their own greed or to make God their servant. I know it is not the cure for every situation, the truth is the only cure for every situation is God Himself and doing what He says to do; however, it is a wonderful way to cooperate with God in reshaping our souls and changing the course of our lives. I am always so glad when I make this a regular part of my devotions, and regret it when I let it slip because it does such a powerful work in my soul, and sometimes even in my body or circumstances.

Chapter 4 • Prayer Proclamations

Like so many truths, there is a learning curve involved in using prayer proclamations well. Some, like me, after hearing a teaching on the power of spoken words, tried practicing Scripture-based confessions. We were disappointed when things did not change as we desired. We spoke to our mountain with all the faith we had, but the mountain did not move. If the result does not come in what we consider a reasonable amount of time, whether a few seconds or a few years, we stop the practice. After all, we are busy people with lots to do and if something is not working, we want to do something that does work instead.

It is helpful to realize there are different levels of proclamations or confessions. One level is "sowing." Jesus said God's word is sown through the spoken word. That is true for sharing God's message with others, and it is true for sowing His word in our own lives. Hearing words audibly spoken can be like sowing the seed, it does not produce noticeable results right away, but speaking it has planted the seed in the soil. Another level is "watering." In 1 Corinthians 3, Paul wrote that he planted the seed and Apollos watered it, but God caused the growth. He was writing about teaching God's truth to the church in Corinth, but the same principle applies to us proclaiming God's word over our lives. It is not enough to simply plant the seed, it has to be nurtured and watered to come to maturity. Regularly confessing God's words, based on what He is doing in our lives, is an important way we water the soil of our hearts and the seed of God's word. Then comes harvest time, and this is where we speak God's word out of our mouth and we see the change take place. In John 4, Jesus referred to the harvest as people coming to faith in Him as the result of hearing the gospel. I have seen over the years, just as the gospel is planted as a seed, then watered, then a person

Section IV—The Practices

eventually comes to a place of faith in Jesus, the same process happens in other areas of our lives. This is the exciting time where either faith has increased to such a degree that we have total assurance that what we have been praying and proclaiming is going to happen, or it just happens as a result of speaking God's words.

There is another level of direction-changing words that goes with the gift of faith. In Mark 11:23 (NASB), Jesus said, "Truly I say to you, whoever says to this mountain, 'Be taken up and cast into the sea,' and does not doubt in his heart, but believes that what he says is going to happen, it will be granted him." Jesus had just cursed a fig tree and, as a result, the tree dried up from the roots. Seeing this demonstration of power, the disciples asked Jesus about it and he told them anyone who speaks with unwavering faith could do the same. Here is the catch though: I do not think human beings, even Spirit-filled believers, have the faith to move mountains without God's specific presence and promise for that situation.

Over the years, I have seen so many sincere Christians speak to circumstances with all the faith they had, whether it be for physical healing or a restored marriage or a financial miracle, and it never happened. They quoted these words of Jesus, but it did not come to pass—the mountain stayed. So is Jesus lying? Does what He says not work? Of course it works; God cannot lie! This type of power through words, though, comes when God gives a special gift of faith for a specific situation. There is no Christian on the planet that can walk around and tell every crippled person they see to get up and walk and have it happen, unless God is specifically giving faith and miracle power for that situation. No Christian can go up to dead people and tell them to come back to life, unless God gives the faith and

Chapter 4 • Prayer Proclamations

power for it. Moses could not part the waters of every river or lake he saw. He could only be used by God to do it when God said to do it. Even Spirit-empowered, full-of-God's-word believers do not have that great of power constantly flowing through them. The potential is there, because this type of faith and power is in God, but this is a gift of the Spirit, released through words or actions given only as God wills. When we understand these different levels of word power, it helps us to use words the way God intends.

Because I have a more introverted personality, one of the battles I have had to face over the years is whether I can be a good pastor/leader/speaker without being a big extrovert. Many successful pastors have that life-of-the-party personality and they seem to have the ability to carry on a conversation with a rock. Sometimes, after hearing a super funny or extroverted speaker, I look at myself and hear words in my mind like, "You should not even be in the ministry. You could never be that way. Go get a job doing something else." So how do I deal with that? Sometimes not very well, and then I get depressed, but when I remember I have a spiritual enemy who knows my weaknesses and tries to make me ineffective, then I start to fight against those thoughts. It is not by simply praying that God would make them stop, because God rarely makes these attacks stop if I just ask Him. It does not help to feel sorry for myself, though sometimes I do. Moreover, it is not by going around fishing for compliments, as people rarely give them during these times anyway. When I wake up to what is happening, I fight these errant thoughts by doing what Jesus did, by using spoken words of Scripture.

In Matthew 4, Jesus was led by the Holy Spirit into the wilderness after His public baptism and after the Holy Spirit came upon Him. He fasted for forty days and, at

Section IV—The Practices

some point, the devil came to tempt Him. This was an incredibly important time, because if Satan could get Jesus to give in to even one temptation and sin, the whole redemption plan was out the window. Only a sinless One could pay the price for our sins. Therefore, Satan used his very best, most impressive temptations on three different occasions. We would do well to notice that Jesus used the same weapon each time the enemy attacked Him. He did not say, "I am the Son of God, go away." He did not just try to ignore the enemy and He did not just think happy thoughts. He did not even pray and ask the Father to stop the enemy's temptations. Every single time, He took the right Scripture and spoke it out of His mouth to Satan. Each time Jesus said, "It is written" and then quoted a Scripture. Ephesians 6:17 calls the word of God "the sword of the Spirit" because it has the power to cut through Satan's lies and temptations. If the Son of God did not depend on his own holiness and right-standing with God to defeat the enemy, but instead He spoke God's words, what does that tell us? We need to speak God's words to defeat the enemy's attacks, to break His strongholds, and to see freedom and release come in our souls.

Therefore, when those attacks come against me and I realize what is going on, I respond during my private time by getting appropriate Scriptures and proclaiming them or statements based on them. I say things like, "God has gifted me, chosen me, and made me according to His plan. He has made it clear through His inner leading, through the confirmation of other leaders, and through fruitfulness that He has called me to serve by leading, equipping, and preaching. I am just right to reach and connect with the people God has called me to reach. I rejoice in the gifts and callings of others, and praise God that they are reaching people

Chapter 4 • Prayer Proclamations

I could not. I will give it my best and trust God to cause maximum impact for His glory and His kingdom." When I proclaim words like that, faith begins to rise in my heart and the lies causing oppression dissipate.

Psalm 45:1 (NASB) says, "My tongue is the pen of a ready writer." With our words we sow, we water, we harvest, we fight the enemy, and we write. Where do we write? We write on our hearts and minds by speaking words. Paul talks about this again in 2 Corinthians 3:3 (NASB) when he writes, "being manifested that you are a letter of Christ, cared for by us, written not with ink, but with the Spirit of the living God, not on tablets of stone but on tablets of human hearts." The Holy Spirit takes God's words and writes them on our hearts. When that happens, they change how we think, believe, talk, and act. The Holy Spirit, however, does not just write them from nothing. He takes the words God has spoken, which were recorded in the Bible, and as we read them, hear them, picture them, or say them, He writes those words on our hearts.

For years, I wondered about passages in the New Testament like Ephesians 6:10–17, which talks about putting on the whole armor of God so we can stand strong against the schemes of the devil. Ephesians and Colossians have several sections that tell us to put off the old sin nature and to put on Christ, or put on Christ-like virtues. I wondered how I was to do that. After years of practice, study, and listening to other teachers, I believe it is mainly by speaking and picturing God's words with as much faith as I presently have. For example, I pray and say, "By faith, Heavenly Father, I now put on the belt of truth, the breastplate of righteousness, and the helmet of salvation. I see myself walking in Your truth which sets me free. I see myself in Jesus righteousness, so there is no room for any condemnation or

Section IV—The Practices

hopelessness. I see myself living a righteous and holy life, defeating sin this day. I see my mind protected by Your divine helmet. I take every thought that goes through my mind today captive to the obedience of Christ. I think in terms of Your salvation and Your solutions in every situation. Negativity, depression, and defeat have no place in my thinking because greater is He who is in me than he who is in the world." What am I doing? I am putting on God's armor, I am clothing myself with Christ, and I am using my tongue to write on the tablet of my heart. The Holy Spirit loves working with God's words and He is actively involved in making it work. It is a powerful, life-changing practice that produces great fruit in everyone who sticks with it.

Let me share this as we finish this chapter. Often, the time we need to do this most, is when we least feel like it. Sometimes the devil attacks our feelings with apathy or hopelessness. It is important we remember that if we keep on sowing and watering, we will eventually reap. So do not grow weary in well-doing. In weary times, we especially need to be aware of what is going on and begin proclaiming God's truth over our lives. At first, you may have absolutely no feelings of faith, hope, or victory, but as you begin speaking or singing with as much or as little faith as you have, the Holy Spirit flames will begin to rise up on the inside of you and you will begin to warm up.

The classic Scriptural example of this is in Acts 16 when Paul and Silas have been beaten, put in prison, and locked in stocks for preaching Jesus. About midnight, Paul and Silas were praying and singing hymns of praise to God, but I guarantee you they did not feel like it. They were in great physical pain and I would not doubt it if the devil was trying to serve them a depression, fear, and self-pity cock-

Chapter 4 • Prayer Proclamations

tail. They understood how it worked though, recognized what was happening, and began making prayer proclamations. Victory rose in their hearts and God brought an earthquake that liberated them and resulted in the salvation of more people. Now, God does not always deliver us from our physical circumstances (sometimes He does but not always), but He will deliver us from the shackles of the heart and mind as we verbalize praise and worship to Him and proclaim His truth.

Chapter 5
Prayer People

After living in the States for a few years, our entire family went back for a visit to Munich. At this phase in his young life, our oldest son was going through a time where he greatly exaggerated the pain of every little bump or injury he had. He was not like that earlier and never has been since, in fact, he has turned into a strong young man. Nevertheless, on our trip we were staying with a woman from the church who had offered to keep us. Janet and I were talking with her in her living room when Brandon started screaming. We were not overly concerned about it because, at this phase in his life, it was a fairly regular occurrence. However, when Janet saw blood all over his thumb she took him into the bathroom to wash it off and check it out. A moment later, she called to me with great earnestness in her voice, "Mark, you better come look at this. I think he has cut off part of his thumb." I immediately went into the

Chapter 5 • Prayer People

bedroom where he had been trying to cut open a new box of Legos, and saw the top part of his thumb laying there on the bed. (I know this is gross, but there is a point I am getting to.) We rushed him to the car and I took off like a racecar driver to the hospital. As we were driving, we were praying in the Spirit, with Brandon crying like crazy. All of a sudden, he stopped crying and was very peaceful. We wondered if he had gone into shock, so Janet asked him if he was all right. He said, "Yes, I'm fine. The pain has stopped."

We got to the emergency room and, amazingly, there were no other people there needing treatment. (If you have ever been to an emergency room, you understand why that is amazing.) They took Brandon immediately and a while later brought him out with the thumb bandaged. They said they had never had a young boy act so bravely and calmly as they took the piece of the thumb we had brought with us and stitched it back on. At church the next day, the entire church prayed for his healing and that the thumb would grow back together.

When we got back to the States, we took Brandon to our pediatrician so he could look at the thumb. He told us, "I guess you know that piece they sowed on will never grow back on the rest of the thumb. The doctors in Germany just stitched it on as a natural band-aid, but it will fall off in a short time." We were really discouraged by his words because the doctors in Germany had told us nothing about this. They just told us they had sown it back on and to keep it bandaged until we got back to the States, but they did not perform microsurgery, which our pediatrician said was necessary in this case. He gave us the name of a specialist who could look at it but told us there was no rush

Section IV—The Practices

since there was really nothing much he could do about it at that point in time.

A few days later, we went to the specialist, still praying for a miracle, but trying to brace ourselves that Brandon may have to live the rest of his life without the top of his thumb. When the doctor took off the final bandage and examined it, he said, "It is growing back together quite nicely. In a short time you will not even be able to tell anything had ever happened." That is exactly the way it went. That once severed piece grew back with the rest of the thumb, and today you have to look closely to even see the very thin scar.

There are several points I want to make from this true story. First, God still does healing miracles today. Sometimes they are pure God, with no human participation at all. Other times, He uses people who pray, preach, or use their medical skills, but He does these things all the time even when they are not widely publicized. Second, God loves it when people pray together in harmony. In Matthew 18:19–20 (NIV) Jesus said, "Again, I tell you that if two of you on earth agree about anything you ask for, it will be done for you by my Father in heaven. For where two or three come together in my name, there am I with them." Our immediate family, Janet, David, and I, prayed for Brandon and our church family prayed for him as well. Third, individual parts only live and function correctly when they are connected to the rest of the body. That piece of Brandon's thumb would have turned hard and dead if it had not been quickly reattached to his body. The same is true of us spiritually. 1 Corinthians 12 tells us Christ's church is His body and we are all individual members of it. To live and function well, we must be connected with other believers in Jesus' church. There is no way around it. In the rest of this

Chapter 5 • Prayer People

chapter, I want to concentrate mainly on points two and three: prayer and connection with Christ's body for life change.

It is impossible to read the Bible with an open mind without seeing that God made us for relationships and community. As author/pastor, Ralph Neighbors, has often said, "Community is the highest form of life because God Himself exists in community; Father, Son, and Holy Spirit." Shortly after God created Adam, He said it is not good for man to be alone. Adam knew it too, so he was thrilled when God created Eve. God instituted family, church, and government because he designed us to live in relationships and community with others. God told Israel they were to be His special people together, and He gave them guidelines for living in community as the people of God. When the son of God took on human form, he quickly surrounded Himself with a small group of men who would become His trainees and His best friends. At the last supper, Jesus said to his disciples, "You are those who have stood by me in my trials." (Luke 22:28 NIV)

God in the flesh appreciated friends who stood with Him during the tough challenges He faced. He could have been a lone ranger, but he knew God's way is community. As soon as Jesus ascended to heaven, 120 joined together in the upper room to wait for the promise of the Holy Spirit. It was not 120 people praying alone in their individual homes, they were all together. When the Holy Spirit came, He filled the entire group at once. When the people in Jerusalem heard the tongues and praises of these 120 people and then Peter preached about Jesus, three thousand more put their faith in Jesus as Messiah. The disciples did not send them on their way telling them to seek God by themselves. Acts 2:41 (NIV) says, "Those who accepted his

Section IV—The Practices

message were baptized, and about three thousand were added to their number that day." They were added to the existing community of 120 believers and, as Acts 2:42–47 describes, they lived life together. Bible study, prayer, communion, fellowship, worship, sharing meals, and reaching out to the community on a continuing basis together was their lifestyle.

If we want to see maximum change happen in our lives we must connect with others who want to grow; prayer people. People who are cultivating God-focused, God-centered lives. There may be extremely rare instances, like being stuck on a deserted island or being in isolation in a prison for the faith, where God gives special grace for someone all alone. Still, by far, the majority of the time God's plan is for us to be connected with other God-seeking, prayer people. I know when I first came to Christ, connecting with others who were serious about following God made all the difference in the world for me. I was a brand new baby in Christ and babies know how to do very few things well. That was certainly true of me, even though I had grown up in church. I was shocked when I started reading the Bible and found out the four gospels were, basically, the same story from slightly different perspectives. I was shocked that the Bible was not a list of do's and don'ts; rather it was about the life Jesus came to give. Like every other baby, I did not know how to do much at all spiritually and I needed a spiritual family. It is in family and spiritual community that we get love, protection, nourishment, support, and real life models of how life works.

I will never forget Del Broersma, the leader of a campus fellowship I attended. Del was a professor at Purdue University who did much more than educate college students. He was such an example of a godly, devoted man of

Chapter 5 • Prayer People

God. He did his job very well. He was diligent and passionate about knowing God deeply, he had a great family, and he was active in ministry. As well as consistently teaching the Bible and being involved in church and campus leadership, he still took time once a week to meet with me and another young Christ-follower where we could ask him questions and talk over issues. I remember telling him one time, "I read about some negative things that some people in the Bible said they hated. I have a problem because I actually like doing some of those things. Is there hope for me?" He gave me a wise and loving answer, letting me know that as I grew closer to Jesus, He would help even my desires change. It helped me so much at that beginning part of my new life in Christ. Being around him and the others who were part of that fellowship made it possible for me to get a good foundation as I not only read and heard what to do, but saw living models of how it should work.

As in so many areas, Jesus is once again our example in relationships. He had different levels of relationships that He intentionally developed and lived. He ministered to large crowds of hundreds and thousands where the relationships were not very deep. Ministry was powerful but there was no way for Him to spend lots of time with thousands of people one on one. He also had seventy or so followers that he spent more time with and sent on some short-term mission trips. He spent even more time with the twelve who were the main leaders that He would build His church on. Then were three who were with Him more than all the others, who became His closest friends and, finally, there was one who was His very best friend (next to His Heavenly Father). We, too, need these different levels of friendship and interaction for maximum growth.

Section IV—The Practices

It helps so much to be a part of the larger crowd, the entire local church, for celebration, worship, teaching, and witness. That level of interaction is one Jesus led people into on a regular basis and is still important today. So many people have had major God encounters in large group settings, but large groups alone do not allow Christianity to be practiced and mastered. For example, it is not enough to hear great teaching or read books on playing a guitar; we must also practice it in order to play it. Christianity is the same way because it is not just head knowledge, it is, even more so, a life to be lived and developed. This can only happen in smaller groups where we can practice living the Christian life. We cannot love in a vacuum.

Along with our time alone with God, we need interaction with other fallen, works-in-progress people to work out the salvation God has given us. It is easy to have nice feelings for people from a distance; it is another thing when we are close enough that they step on our toes or say something that hurts us. It is in these settings, we learn to love like Jesus loves us, to forgive, and to appreciate other types of people. We cannot develop this simply by going to a larger group service. Getting together with others on a regular basis, in smaller groups, is essential to grow into Christlikeness.

All the levels of community Jesus modeled should be our goal because we need all of them. People get it wrong when they think we need to have deep, intimate relationships with everyone in the church. Several years ago, when we started a new church, some sincere women kept coming to me telling me that we needed to get super close with those attending before we started to reach out to others. They said we need to have those deep relationships with everyone in the church like they had in the New Testament.

Chapter 5 • Prayer People

If we did that, God would just add people to the church; we would not even need to reach out to the lost because God would just do it. Even in Germany, sometimes people would tell me that we needed to get deeper with each other, with everyone, before we reach out to the lost around us. After thinking about it, looking at Scripture, and praying about it, I realized a few things.

First, people do have the need for strong friendships. Second, it is true if we love each other the way Jesus said, people would know we are His disciples, and this would be a great witness to those around us (John 13:34–35). Third, to be super close with everyone in the church was not only impossible, it was also not even Jesus' practice. Super close friendships and relationships will be with just a few people and that is fine. It is biblical to have different levels of friendship and relationship. Fourth, if we want to be close to each other, we need to be doing what Jesus wants done, which is to reach out to the lost. If we will reach up, reach in, and reach out, we will have far stronger relationships than just reaching up and in. Some of those people saw what I was saying and stuck with us; others went on their way looking for the super deep relational church and are still looking today because it does not exist. It is good to have different levels of community.

What is the best way to find people like this to connect with? Look at your interests, needs, or passions at this time in your life. Are you most interested in knowing the Bible better, or managing your finances, or working through a personal problem? We are most open to learning and changing when we are interested in the topic. So, find a group that is doing what you are interested in at this time. You can change to another group when your interests change. I was never interested in parenting until I had kids.

Section IV—The Practices

Forcing me to go to a parenting class would have been pointless when I was eighteen years old because I would not have paid attention at all. However, once I had a child, then I was interested because my life had changed. If we give people freedom to do what they are interested in at that particular time in their life, they will learn more and develop friendships more easily than forcing everyone in the church to all do the same thing. I believe in small group involvement, but even with regular small group participation, we need to realize there will be different levels of friendship that develop. We may really click with some in a group, others we will just be nice to, and still others that we will have to force ourselves to love, at least for a while. It is amazing how God can help us love people with sandpaper personalities. All of that is biblical. We need those different levels of community to help us grow up in "all aspects into Christ." (Ephesians 4:15)

The two main factors in how much a group has an impact on us are how often we have interaction with each other, and how open we are to others in the group. Just like our relationship with God, if we are consistent in our time with God and we open our lives up, then the receptivity of our souls increases greatly. Support recovery groups are so effective because they get together consistently and they open their hearts wide to each other. They have reached the point where they no longer care if people know about their problems and struggles, they just want help. With a wide-open heart, God works and the influence of God through others is multiplied. We all know the difference between being closed or open to others. If we are closed, even if what they say or do is right and said with great love, we will block it completely and it will have little or no impact on us. If, however, the trust or desperation level is high

Chapter 5 • Prayer People

enough to open the gates of our hearts, Holy Spirit love, truth, and power can flow from one member to another and provide great help.

That, of course, means you want to make sure you are opening your life to the right people. It normally takes some time to develop the kind of trust that opens our hearts, but keep praying and working at developing it. Sow seeds of friendship with different people and groups, and see which ones start to grow and sprout. There are definitely people out there you will connect with and can be of great support to you and you to them.

Along with large group church participation, I am also always involved with some type of small group. The early church met in the temple and from house to house, following Jesus example. Each Christian would do well to follow that example also. In one small group I am currently involved in, I meet with three other men for the specific goals of personal and leadership growth. We talk over goals and issues, which help stir us up and encourage us to stay at it. The more we open up to each other, the greater the level of impact our times together have. Sharing, talking, and interacting are powerful means for life change, especially when combined with believing prayer.

The longer I walk with God, the more I am convinced that one of the greatest means of growth and change, which is too seldom taken advantage of, is dedicated prayer for each other. When I read Paul's letters, I cannot help but see how often and fervently he prayed for the churches he started and for individuals in those churches. The prayers recorded in his letters are rich with insight on how spiritual growth works since Paul had an incredibly deep understanding of the process. With all he had to do, Paul still made lots of time to pray these rich prayers for others be-

Section IV—The Practices

cause he understood what a powerful effect they had. He sincerely believed that what he prayed would play a big role in how those people developed. He really believed God would take the words he prayed and use them as material for building into the prayer recipient's lives. Paul did not write prayers that said, "Lord, just bless them. Lord, You know what they need so give it to them." Those types of prayers do help, but Paul prayed rich, specific prayers like Colossians 1:9–12 (NIV), "For this reason, since the day we heard about you, we have not stopped praying for you and asking God to fill you with the knowledge of his will through all spiritual wisdom and understanding. And we pray this in order that you may live a life worthy of the Lord and may please him in every way: bearing fruit in every good work, growing in the knowledge of God, being strengthened with all power according to his glorious might so that you may have great endurance and patience, and joyfully giving thanks to the Father, who has qualified you to share in the inheritance of the saints in the kingdom of light." Paul is obviously using this prayer as a teaching point, but this is also how he actually prayed. The only reason he would pray so richly, so specifically, is because he believed God heard and would use his prayers, the words he spoke to God, to help it come to pass.

Once again, the faith factor is really big in how dedicated we are to prayer and receiving prayer. If I think the only thing prayer does is somehow change me, then praying those apostolic type of prayers for others is not really needed. I could just meditate on the words, or worship, or fellowship with God. But if I believe the words I pray matter, and God does listen to our prayers and uses our words, then those types of prayers make sense. Not only that, it can turn intercessory prayer and prayers of petition into an

Chapter 5 • Prayer People

energizing time, rather than a dull, boring duty. When I believe God is taking my prayers and using them to change things, it motivates me to pray. Revelation 8:3–5, and several other Scriptures, show us that God takes our prayers and uses them to bring change on the earth.

So imagine, not only are you doing your part to cooperate with God for life change, you are also getting others to pray for you. Because He knew the power of prayer, Paul regularly asked churches to pray for him. Jesus said if two or three agree in prayer, God does it! Unity, especially in prayer, does not just add, it multiplies, grace and power. That is why Paul took his prayers so seriously and why we should too. Find and join with prayer people to partner with God in life change.

As we finish our time together, I think it would be appropriate and helpful to let me do a little Paul-like praying for you based on the main points of this book.

Here is my prayer for you.

> I pray, in the name of Jesus, that God would:
> Help you get in His River of Life and give you real hope that you can change.
> Teach you how to walk with trust in Him while you give it your best.
> Fill you with Holy Spirit revelation.
> Keep you anchored in foundational truth.
> Help you sing the song of heaven, with Jesus as your number one.
> Cause you to know Jesus deeply and hear His voice clearly.
> Keep filling you with Holy Spirit power.
> Enable you to set your mind on the things of the Spirit.

Section IV—The Practices

Make clear to you the Holy Spirit's leading at every stage of life.

Give you a great hunger for His word.

Open your heart to receive His word by faith.

Give you patience and determination in seasons of delay.

Strengthen you to stand strong against the enemy.

Draw you to become a person of His presence in prayer.

Make His plans clear to you.

Give you biblical, Spirit-inspired pictures to focus on.

Free you to use His words wisely.

Join you to the right people.

That you may grow from barrenness to fruitfulness, add what is lacking, and live a significant, fulfilling, God-glorifying life.

Amen.

References

Guillen, Michael. 1995. *Five equations that changed the world.* New York: Hyperion.

Holy Bible, New Living Translation, Tyndale Charitable Trust.

The Holy Bible, New International Version, Zondervan Publishing House.

New American Standard Bible, The Lockman Foundation.

The Message, Nav Press.

The New Testament, New Century Version, Word Publishing.

Warren, Rick. 2002. *The Purpose Driven Life*. Zondervan Publishing House.

LaVergne, TN USA
31 August 2009
156464LV00003B/6/P